BECOMING PRESIDENT

*Patterns of Professional Mobility of
African American University Presidents*

Jyotsna Mishra

University Press of America,® Inc.
Lanham · Boulder · New York · Toronto · Plymouth, UK

Copyright © 2007 by
University Press of America,® Inc.
4501 Forbes Boulevard
Suite 200
Lanham, Maryland 20706
UPA Acquisitions Department (301) 459-3366

Estover Road
Plymouth PL6 7PY
United Kingdom

All rights reserved
Printed in the United States of America
British Library Cataloging in Publication Information Available

Library of Congress Control Number: 2006933312
ISBN-13: 978-0-7618-3628-5 (paperback : alk. paper)
ISBN-10: 0-7618-3628-4 (paperback : alk. paper)

∞™ The paper used in this publication meets the minimum
requirements of American National Standard for Information
Sciences—Permanence of Paper for Printed Library Materials,
ANSI Z39.48—1984

In loving memory of my mother who, without any formal education of her own, appreciated the value of education, particularly for women, and encouraged all of us in that direction.

Contents

Figures	vii
Tables	ix
Preface	xi
1. Introduction	1
2. Review of Literature	11
3. Methodology	31
4. Analysis of Data	37
5. Summary, Conclusions, Implications, and Recommendations	59
References	73
Index	81

Figures

4.1	Current age of African American HBCU and TWI presidents	48
4.2	Age at presidency of African American HBCU and TWI presidents	49
4.3	Region of birth for African American HBCU and TWI presidents	49
4.4	Gender of African American HBCU and TWI presidents	50
4.5	Institutions at which presidents earned their bachelor's degree	50
4.6	Institutions at which presidents earned their terminal degree	51
4.7	Type of terminal degree earned by African American presidents	52
4.8	Professional experience at HBCUs	52
4.9	Professional experience at non-HBCUs	53
4.10	Entry position for African American presidents	53
4.11	First administrative position for African American presidents	54
4.12	Last position before presidency for African American presidents	54
4.13	Leadership positions in civic and professional organizations	55

Tables

3.1	Definitions of different mobility rates	32
4.1	Demographic profile of African American presidents of HBCUs	38
4.2.	Educational profile for African American presidents of HBCUs	40
4.3	Career related characteristics of African American presidents of HBCUs	41
4.4	Relationship between academic discipline and mobility	43
4.5	Summary of gender and academic discipline	44
4.6	Relationship between gender and mobility	44
4.7	Relationship between additional training and mobility	45
4.8	Relationship between marital status and mobility	46
4.9	Relationship between age at presidency and mobility	46
4.10	Relationship between region of origin and mobility	47
4.11	Summary of presidents' position of entry into career and mobility	47
4.12	Relationship between institutional types and upward mobility	56
4.13	Relationship between gender and mobility for TWI presidents	56
4.14	Relationship between marital status and mobility for TWI presidents	57
4.15	Relationship between gender and marital status of African American presidents of TWIs	57

Preface

This book is intended to offer a small contribution to the growing literature on patterns of professional mobility of African American college and university presidents in United States. One major purpose is to help both higher education stakeholders and community leaders to envision the career patterns of these educators in their rise to the presidency. I conducted this research as part of my work toward an advanced academic degree in educational leadership at Samford University. However, my academic interest in this area stems from my long faculty tenure in a historically black college where I was committed to exploring the leadership roles and professional management patterns of African American presidents in historically black colleges and universities. My commitment to the success of these unique institutions has always been a profound and personal one.

Prior to this book's publication, Dr. Albert J.H. Sloan, II, the beloved president of Miles College, died. His passing poignantly reminded me that the meaning of a college president's career and life has much to do with the way that president touched others. This is especially true of an academic leader like Dr. Sloan, whose influence reached students, colleagues and the community, and whose legacy reaches into the future.

Several important sources of inspiration, support, and assistance have made possible my venture to write this book. First, I would like to acknowledge Dr. Maurice Persall for guiding and supporting me in my research. I would also like to thank Dr. Angela Owusu-Ansah for her incredible patience in directing me toward the most appropriate research design. Dr. Sarah Johnson, a longtime friend and colleague, was gracious with her time and energy in reading the manuscript and making valued suggestions. Dr. Geraldine Bell, Director of the Kirkendoll Learning Resource Center at Miles College, provided tremendous help in making library resources at Miles College available for my research. Several colleagues on the Miles College Social and Behavioral Sciences faculty are due profound thanks. Dr. Beverly Hawk read the manuscript with her characteristic rigor and humor and offered rich insights into methodology and style. Dr. Jerome Green, who in addition to his faculty position serves as an attorney for the African Methodist Episcopal Church, set me straight on the role of the AME Church in providing higher education for African Americans. I am deeply indebted to my friend and colleague, Jill Miller, for her countless hours formatting and editing the manuscript.

I am grateful to the late Dr. Albert J. H. Sloan, II and Dr. Hattie G. Lamar for offering a Lilly Grant fellowship to work on my Ph.D. I am very appreciative of Dr. Ruth Ash for recommending the Samford University doctoral program in educational leadership. I also hold in special remembrance the late Dr. Manindra Kumar Mohapatra of Indiana State University, a longtime family friend and co-author of *Beyond September 11, 2001: Political Attitudes of Indian Immigrants in America* for initially suggesting this research topic and methodology.

My foremost gratitude goes to my family. My late father, Ram Chandra Mishra, my eldest brother, Madhu Sudan Mishra (the first college graduate in the family), and his wife, Usha Mishra, raised and supported me throughout my life. According to family lore, our mother was so impressed with the demeanor of a professional female nurse treating her that she wished for me to receive an education to earn such a professional standing. I am deeply indebted to my brother for respecting my mother's last wish and giving me the opportunity to fulfill this wish.

I have been fortunate to receive extraordinary support from my husband, Digambar Mishra. He has always challenged and motivated me to pursue my academic and professional dreams. His unwavering commitment has enabled us to complete our degrees, become tenured faculty in our professions, and raise a great family. I must thank him and our wonderful children, Anoop and Likun, for their grace, patience, support, encouragement, and assistance from the beginning. Finally, I thank God for giving me the opportunities and guidance to achieve my goals, personally and professionally.

In acknowledging the contributions of love, inspiration, encouragement, and assistance, for which I am extremely grateful, I must also acknowledge that any shortcomings of this work are my own.

Jyotsna Mishra
Birmingham, Alabama

July, 2006

Chapter 1

Introduction

The modern presidency in higher education has evolved into a more demanding, complex, and serious role in recent years. The application of certain criteria is crucial to proper analysis of presidential success. These include longevity, pattern of mobility, and the support system on which the success of a president depends (Hahn 1995). Hahn considers these criteria to logically, though not perfectly, correlate to the leadership effectiveness and success of a university president. He further recommends a thorough and careful examination of these correlates while investigating presidential success.

Rhodes (1998) views the presidency as the most influential of all positions in higher education communities. He defines those communities as comprising the boards of directors or trustees, administrators, faculty, students, and parents. Unlike in European and Asian institutions where the president or vice-chancellor is without true executive authority, the American higher education president is the chief executive officer with ultimate authority for all decisions made within the institution (Duderstadt 2000a). In addition, Duderstadt (2000a) states that the office of the president is critically important in directing the mission, structure, budget, and personnel of higher education institutions during these times of change. Changes in higher education reflect changes in society (Bok 1998). According to Cunningham (1992), institutions of higher education play an important role in addressing societal changes in population demographics, challenges of integration, and diversity. Such changes have been dynamic during the last decades of the twentieth century.

Although the Hispanic population is the fastest growing minority group in America, African Americans still comprise the largest minority ethnic group in the country. However, African Americans are still underrepresented in high-level administrative positions in institutions of higher education. Of the 2,400 institutions of higher education that exist in the United States, only 156 African Americans hold positions of president or provost (Wilson 1996).

African American University presidents are often the chief administrators of historically black colleges and universities (HBCUs) in America and are reported to be under greater pressure than their white counterparts in traditionally white institutions (TWIs). This discrepancy in pressure extends primarily from the lower financial bases with which HBCUs must function compared to TWIs (Scott 2002). Former U.S. Congressman Watts, who heads the HBCU Initiative under the Bush administration, stated that "Most of the HBCUs just do not have that kind of alumni capacity and that kind of community capacity to meet those kinds of needs or challenges," (Watts, personal communication).

Despite these obstacles faced by African American university presidents, substantial changes in the last two decades have enabled HBCUs to not only survive, but also to reach new heights in institutional management. For example, the new generation of presidents selected within the last five years have come from a talented and diverse pool of leaders across various disciplines in higher education (New Black College Presidents 1999). According to Bennett (1991), these presidents are expected to have "the organizational skills of a field marshal, the fiscal acumen of a CPA, the diplomacy of a politician and the vision of a prophet" (p. 27). In view of the importance of HBCUs in higher education, particularly in the face of societal changes and challenges, the role of the university president as an effective leader (Rhodes 1998) has been vital to the success of HBCUs.

According to Hahn (1995) longevity, patterns of mobility, and support systems of university presidents play pivotal roles in the success of university presidents. This study seeks to investigate the success of African American university presidents by examining the trends and patterns of upward mobility through the identification of multi-dimensional traits and characteristics. The study also seeks to determine whether mobility rates are impacted by certain personal and professional characteristics. According to Fincher (1997), the personal qualities and professional experiences of individual leaders interact with organizational structure to produce a desired outcome. Vardi (1980) developed a career mobility model in which the mobility rates are dependent variables and individual characteristics are predictors. In this study, mobility rates similarly serve as the dependent variables while professional and individual characteristics are used as predictors (independent variables).

Theoretical Framework

Professional mobility for this study is concerned with career mobility within the administrative hierarchy. Therefore, some theories pertaining to career mobility, as they relate to administration in institutions of higher education and certain institutional structures, are examined. No one theory, however, seems to be perfectly aligned with the administrative career mobility of HBCU presidents. The majority of research on administrative careers is limited to personal experiences in upward mobility of senior level administrators.

The career pattern of administrators is not as clearly delineated in higher education as that of the faculty career ladder which is well structured (Twombly 1986a). Cohen and March (1974) identified a normative career ladder for the presidency of a higher education institution to be comprised of various administrative positions in sequence starting with a faculty position. However, studies that used this normative ladder found numerous deviations. Furthermore, there appears to be no significant research relative to administrative mobility of senior administrators in four-year institutions of higher education. Moore, Martorana, and Twombly (1985) attempted to study administrative mobility in two-year institutions of higher education by placing particular emphasis on careers as structures of organizations and utilizing the internal labor market theory as an analytical framework.

Twombly (1986b) used models which focused on the individual level of analysis and the organizational-structural level of analysis. The individual level of analysis considers factors which are based on psychological and sociological concepts. Sociological concepts deal with individual characteristics, career patterns, and career behavior (Vardi 1980). The organizational level of analysis highlights administrative and economic concepts. Economic concepts involve utilizing the internal labor market theory for studying organizational careers (Vardi 1980). Studies examining administrative careers within higher education have shown that the mobility of administrators is influenced by structural variables such as region, institutional types, prior position, and resource level.

Clearly, the separation of individual characteristics from structural elements can prove to be difficult. In fact, the interaction between opportunity structures and an individual worker's resources seems to be very appropriate when mobility in institutions of higher education is concerned. This constitutes several mobility models including the model of labor market segmentation. Internal labor market theory is a part of this model. The key characteristic of this market is the progressive advancement towards more responsible tasks and positions (Althauser 1989).

Statement of the Problem

Presidents of institutions of higher education, whether public or private, four-year or two-year, colleges or universities, are challenged to have a vision for the future in these uncertain times. They are plagued by limited resources arising from budget cuts, historically low returns on investments in stocks and bonds, and general faculty and administrator apathy due to lack of competitive salary structures, low quality curricula, and problems of grade inflation (Fisher and Tack 1990).

According to recent reports published in *Academe* (The historically black colleges, 1995), *Ebony* (Black college presidents, 2001), and the *Salt Lake Tribune* (Scott 2002), historically black colleges and universities continue to struggle with issues of public and private support, mergers, and possible closures. These reports also state that in the past five years, about a quarter of the nation's historically black colleges and universities have lost presidents due to growing internal and external pressures in dealing with the above complex issues.

While HBCU presidents have taken bold steps to deal with diversity, competition, technology needs, and community skepticism toward race relations, predominantly white universities continue to explore ways to increase and retain qualified African American administrators to promote diversity and affirmative action. *Ebony* (New black college presidents 1999) reports that the new generation of black college presidents—highly trained, technologically oriented, and managerially adept—have introduced a new style of leadership to college campuses. These new presidents have held positions not only as educators but also as scientists, corporate executives, government officials, and even television personalities. In the face of increasingly formidable challenges these leaders must have vision to meet the task of educating African American students.

In challenging times like the current period facing HBCU presidents, it is especially appropriate and necessary to explore the reasons for presidential success by identifying common biographical traits and characteristics that are associated with upward mobility, and examining the impact of certain characteristics on the rate of upward mobility.

Most would acknowledge that African American presidents of historically black colleges and universities have earned the reputation of serving as inspirational role models for African American students, faculties, and administrators (Phelps, Taber, and Smith 1996). In a report published by the Department of Education (*White House Initiative* 1997), President Bill Clinton commented:

> Historically black colleges and universities continue to play a vital role by adding to the diversity and caliber of the Nation's higher education system. Furthermore, these institutions remind all Americans of our obligations to uphold the principles of justice and equality enshrined in our Constitution. (P. 3)

Purpose of the Study

As stated earlier, the issues and challenges of today's institutions of the higher education, regardless of their demographics and clientele, demand unique skills, traits, and experiences of the presidents to move the respective institutions forward (Barwick 2002). Although American higher education generally has experienced a tremendous amount of success on a global scale, university presidents have been subjected to criticism, questioning, and skepticism (Birnbaum 1999).

Undoubtedly, the president's job in higher education must be taken seriously and certain criteria including patterns of mobility and support systems must be thoroughly analyzed in order to unearth the roots of presidential success (Hahn 1995). Studies pertaining to the qualities, attributes, traits, and characteristics that impact the career mobility of presidents may provide valuable insights into their paths of success. These studies must equally weigh consideration of the president's role within the context of the cultural milieu in which they are situated.

The overall purpose of this study has three objectives. The study intends to: (a) identify and examine the relationship between the rate of upward professional mobility among African American university presidents and certain biographical predictor variables in demographic, social, educational, occupational, and organizational dimensions; (b) examine the pattern of mobility by determining the common traits and behaviors of African American presidents who have apparently reached the top of their career ladder; (c) examine the differences or similarities between African American presidents of historically black colleges and universities and the African American presidents of traditionally white institutions in terms of the relationship between biographical predictors and professional mobility.

In this process, the study utilizes only unobtrusive biographical data for analysis. This is a departure from typical survey data used in studies about administrators of institutions of higher education. The data are collected from public archival sources.

Although African American university presidents constitute the participants of this study, special emphasis is placed on HBCU presidents since a significant number of African American presidents in higher education serve HBCUs.

Research Questions

This study attempts to answer the following questions:

1. Are there commonalities in specific demographic, educational, and career profiles of the African American presidents in historically black colleges and universities? If so, what are they?

2. Is there a relationship between the educational disciplines of African American presidents of historically black colleges and universities and their upward professional mobility?

3. Is there a gender-based difference among presidents of historically black colleges and universities in terms of (a) training in certain academic disciplines and (b) the rate of upward mobility?

4. Do African American presidents of historically black colleges and universities with additional study/training beyond their degree of discipline ascend the administrative career ladder faster than those without?

5. Is there a difference in the upward mobility of African American presidents of historically black colleges and universities with regard to (a) marital status, (b) age, and (c) region of origin?

6. Is there a relationship between the position of entry in professional career of African American presidents of HBCUs and their upward mobility?

7. What differentiates African American presidents of historically black colleges and universities from African American presidents of traditionally white institutions in terms of upward professional mobility?

Hypotheses

The following hypotheses were tested at the .05 level of significance:

There will be no statistically significant relationship between the educational disciplines of African American presidents of historically black colleges and universities and their upward professional mobility.

There will be no statistically significant gender-based difference among presidents of historically black colleges and universities in terms of (a) training in certain academic disciplines and (b) the rate of upward mobility.

There will be no statistically significant difference in the rate of ascension of African American presidents of historically black colleges and universities with additional study/training beyond their degree of discipline and those without.

There will be no statistically significant difference in the upward mobility of African American presidents of historically black colleges and universities with regard to (a) marital status, (b) age, and (c) state of origin.

There will be no statistically significant relationship between the position of entry in professional career of African American presidents of historically black colleges and universities and their upward mobility.

There will be no statistically significant difference in upward professional mobility between African American presidents of historically black colleges and universities and African American presidents of traditionally white institutions.

Definitions

The following definitions were used for this study.

Career: A succession of related jobs, arranged in hierarchy, through which persons move in more or less predictable sequence (Wilensky 1960).

Mobility: Movement in the career hierarchy.

Career mobility: Progression from one position/job to another in a hierarchy in a profession.

Professional mobility: Mobility in the administrative career hierarchy of academia.

Upward professional mobility: Rate of career progression within the administrative hierarchy of academia.

Unobtrusive measures: Non-reactive methods of gathering data; that is, a means of obtaining data in which subjects are not aware of being studied (Sechrest 1980).

Historically black college and university (HBCU): Institutions that were established prior to 1964, whose principal mission historically has been to educate African-Americans.

National Association for Equal Opportunity (NAFEO) in higher education: An association that represents and supports HBCUs through its contributions in research and policy issues.

Who's Who among African Americans: Annual biographical directory and the most comprehensive publication devoted to recording the accomplishments of successful African Americans in various professions.

Assumptions

1. Self reported biographical data based on voluntary participation of university presidents are reliable and objective. College presidents, with high visi-

bility in their academic and professional communities, would only provide accurate and valid biographical information if they choose to participate.

2. Generally speaking, the credentials of the presidents of the private and public community colleges and presidents of four-year colleges in higher education are not significantly different.

3. The presidents have achieved their positions through a process of upward mobility in their careers.

Delimitation of the Study

The subjects for this study are delimited to African Americans who are currently serving as the chief executive officers of the historically black colleges and universities and African American presidents who are serving traditionally white universities.

Limitation of the Study

There is a possibility that information on specific biographical variables may be missing or incomplete, affecting the result of the study. Also, there is a chance that some information about HBCU presidents may be inaccurately reported or that information on some African American presidents of HBCUs was not available.

Significance of the Study

The state of the presidency in the institution of higher education today is complex and of an urgent concern (Birnbaum 1999; Hahn 1995). According to Hahn, selection of presidents in colleges and universities is a serious job and requires certain criteria to be applied for the analysis of their success. This study seeks to provide insights into the presidential selection process, which is primarily initiated by a board of trustees.

The majority of African American college and university presidents, particularly those who serve at HBCUs, are confronted with additional pressures and challenges because of limited resources in these institutions. These presidents engage in the difficult task of juggling various roles, including that of an administrator, teacher, public relations agent, and civil rights leader (Black college presidents 2001).

Historically black colleges and universities have served as catalysts for providing educational opportunities to generations of African Americans (Frierson 1993). These institutions also serve an increasing number of white, Hispanic, and Asian students (Richmond, Peggy, and Maramark 1996). In addition, historically black colleges and universities tend to have a greater positive impact on African American students and administrators than their white counterparts. HBCUs provide students with a sense of belonging and motivation to focus on professional mobility.

African American presidents have prepared many academic leaders who have played a significant role in the development of past and future leaders. However, there are still very few African American leaders in higher education. In fact, the American Council on Education reported that the number of African American presidents increased by only six percent in the 1990s (Ross and Green 1998). This study may be useful to those who aspire to progress within the administrative career hierarchy to become a leader of the future.

Given the importance of historically black colleges and universities and their presidential leaders for young African American men and women, it is unfortunate that there is a limited volume of studies on African American presidents. Even so, the studies do not focus on the professional or career mobility of these elite academic leaders. Moreover, most of the existing research studies tend to be qualitative only, based primarily on anecdotal evidence coming from interviews.

This study attempts to augment the existing literature on the career mobility of African American presidents in institutions of higher education as well as HBCUs specifically. Through quantitative and qualitative analysis, this study intends to offer insights into the mobility rates and patterns of African American university presidents in their administrative careers by identifying and examining key individual characteristics along personal and professional dimensions. According to Nicholson and West (1988), careers are the balance between innovation and motivation.

This study may further inform African American students and motivate them to consider options for selecting and clarifying career goals and nurturing their individual and collective potential for future leadership. A better understanding of success factors for top level African American administrators in higher education may be valuable in inspiring and leading young African Americans to grow and fulfill their quest for success (Lamb 1989).

Objective and reliable data used in this study are expected to assist in heightening awareness of African American presidents among African American and white educators alike. Hopefully this will translate into the promotion of greater diversity on all college campuses.

Furthermore, this study may provide the current presidents of historically black colleges and universities, regardless of their experiences in these institutions, with a better understanding of their role as leaders in the 21st century. This is particularly relevant at a time when the lack of longevity of the presidents of these institutions seems to be a problem (Suggs 1997).

The methodological significance of using unobtrusive data in conducting research for this study cannot be over-emphasized. Most studies about college presidents are based on survey and interviews. An unobtrusive method involves obtaining information in which subjects are not aware that they are being studied (Bouchard 1976). Hyman (1972) described the use of this method as resourceful use of data generated to address research questions across disciplines. More importantly, data sources used in this study include self-reported biographical data which are objective data provided by college presidents on a voluntary basis.

This study promotes an optimal use of much of the information available across disciplines in data archives. By using archived data, this study may encourage administrators of various institutions to actively participate in the data gathering process, thereby contributing to the development of a broader information database.

Chapter 2

Review of Literature

There is a dearth of literature on upward professional mobility, defined in this study as mobility in the administrative career of a college president or senior level African American college administrator in higher education. The limited availability of information in this specific field is consistent with the more general "paucity of research regarding minority populations and their participation in educational administration" (Valverde and Brown 1988, 144). Literature on the career mobility and progression of historically black college administrators or presidents is even more scarce. This study will add to the current literature on African American presidents, especially those at historically black colleges and universities.

This chapter presents a review of the available literature on career-related areas such as career paths, career mobility, career achievement, glass ceilings, discrimination and internal labor market theory that pertain to African American presidents and administrators at HBCUs. More specifically, this chapter reviews the literature that bear relevance on the traits, characteristics, and factors that affect African American presidents of HBCUs in terms of upward mobility or progression in administrative careers.

In setting the stage for the research questions for this study and establishing a baseline of understanding, relevant literature will be presented in the following five areas:
   a) Presidents in higher education
   b) Women and minority presidents in higher education
   c) Historically black colleges and universities
   d) HBCU presidents
   e) Conceptual/theoretical framework: Career mobility and internal labor market theory

Presidents in Higher Education

The American college presidency began with the election of Henry Dunster as chief officer at Harvard College in 1640 (Fincher 1997). In 1967, the American Council of Education and the Association of Governing Boards of Universities and Colleges defined the president as the Chief Executive Officer (CEO) of an institution of higher education. The role of CEO has continued to evolve over the years. In the formative years of colleges/universities, CEOs were mostly ministers, long-term faculty members, and public relations specialists (Kauffman 1980). According to Kauffman, they were perceived to be the central and essential figures of the institution. Furthermore, a president was perceived to constitute the moral and ethical backbone of an institution of higher education. There is no definitive description of the CEO role because the presidency is continuously evolving (Fisher 1984).

The presidency in higher education today is both distinctive and complex. Unlike in Europe and Asia where the president or vice-chancellor is without true executive authority, the American president is the CEO with ultimate authority for all decisions made within the institution (Duderstadt 2000a). Although presidents traditionally serve "at the pleasure" of a public or private board of trustees, institutional statutes or by-laws commonly identify the president as the chief executive officer and the board delegates to the president all powers necessary to perform those functions (Birnbaum 1999). Birnbaum, however, acknowledges that the presidential influence, in reality, is quite different. As one president commented:

> Regardless of what may appear in the charter and by-laws, the authority of the president and his real leadership depends on the willingness of the campus to accept him as a leader. If it will not, well there are other ways for him to earn a living. (P. 326)

Presidents in institutions of higher education have undergone revolutionary transformations in the past thirty years, in response to profound social, economic, and technological changes in society. The challenges they have confronted include budget cutbacks, curricular changes, shifts in student profiles, educational technology, dynamic organizational structures, changes in governmental influence, and state/local political pressures (Duderstadt 2000b; Gleason 2000; Jusman 1999; Penny 1996; Shea 2003).

Rachel Hartigan Shea (2003), writing for *U.S. News and World Report*, characterized the decades that have passed since 1983, when that publication began ranking colleges, as "tumultuous for higher education" (p. 76). She catalogued the changes that occurred during those years as follows:

> Professors, administrators, and their critics have fought pitched battles over "political correctness" inside and outside the classroom; new academic fields like genomics and postcolonial studies have opened up; and more people than ever before have signed on for a college education. Meanwhile, the ivory tower has been scaled by powerful market forces as financial realities have forced colleges to embrace such previously foreign concepts as "return on investment," "customer service," and "branding." (p. 76)

From a more forward-looking and administrative perspective, James W. Duderstadt (2000b) explored and analyzed some of these ongoing process changes in his book *A University for the 21st Century*. According to Duderstadt, President Emeritus and University Professor of Science and Engineering at the University of Michigan, the increase in the complexity of a university calls for the recognition of the importance of modern university presidential leadership.

In a lecture for the Digital Future Seminar at Emory University, Duderstadt argued that change must not be driven by economic forces alone. The broader purpose of the university, which he defined as the mission to preserve and convey heritage and to be a social critic, must be kept in mind. He saw technological changes as a driving force, as universities scramble to serve a new generation of students inculcated in the digital age. He also emphasized the need of a strategic framework to steer the future university (Gleason 2000).

In a report published in *Educational Record* (Penney 1996), Sherry Penney, the Chancellor of the University of Massachusetts at Boston, describes the demands that will be placed on academic leaders of the 21st century as follows:

> I see five specific challenges for academic leaders as we prepare for tomorrow's turbulent world. They are the necessity to: manage and enhance change; reassert academic leadership; balance an institution's many and varied constituencies; raise increasing amount of funds; and respond to increasing demands for strict accountability. Because of these five challenges, we will serve in an academic world that bears little resemblance to what is so familiar to us today. (P. 19)

These emerging challenges simply add to the traditional challenges that university presidents have faced. Pre-eminent among these challenges is establishing a leadership mandate amidst faculty control. Presidents continue to battle the perceived and real powers afforded to faculty within institutions of higher education, powers that may seemingly constrain presidential initiative (Griffiths 1988). It has been said that "University faculties have systematically made it impossible (or nearly so) for deans and presidents to lead or to administer, and the better the university, the less it is led" (Griffiths 1988, 37). According to James Fairweather (1996),

> The challenge for academic leaders is to fulfill traditional functions well, to meet new challenges at the same time, and to accomplish these tasks without losing the managerial authority. Indeed, Clark Kerr went so far as to say that the key to innovation lies in the battleground between administrative leadership and faculty conservatism. (Pp. 5-6)

The modern university presidency has also witnessed an increase in pressure from external sources and environment. In a survey of 216 presidents of four-year institutions, respondents noted, "The state legislature, the governor, the state board of education, the state budget office, and professional and regional accrediting agencies have the most influence on their decision-making" (Evangelauf 1984, 15).

Undoubtedly, contemporary presidents of colleges and universities are expected to play multiple roles, including chief administrator of a complex bureaucracy, mentor of a professional community, public official accountable to an educational board, fiscal manager, recruiter, public relations officer, and fund raiser (Birnbaum 1999; Hahn 1995).

The multiple constituencies mandate that college presidents possess a clear vision of the complexity of their organizations, including the macro and micro levels of analysis from which to establish an "informed" direction (Lewin and Regine 2001). The paradoxical leadership model addresses this particular need. According to Lewin and Regine, "Paradoxical leadership fluctuates at the edge of a mechanistic and organic style of leadership, between structure and less structure, and in the world of complexity, fluctuation is healthy" (p. 271). They continue their description of this model:

> Paradoxical leadership incorporates both the need for a leader to be strong, in terms of a strong sense of direction, a clear sense of self, and definitive values, and also an ability to let go, be open-ended, and to allow the organization to evolve, to respect that development, and let it take its own course. Both guidance and open-endedness are needed to lead in complex adaptive systems. . . . The fundamental paradox in this leadership style is being *leaders by not leading*. (P. 272)

As college presidents contend with and attempt to balance numerous, often conflicting internal and external interests in this era, the successful leaders will be able to handle "paradoxes" that create tensions from which creative and productive solutions can arise (Lewin and Regine 2001). In fact, Lewin and Regine believe not only that paradoxes "are something to embrace, to contain," but also that "seeing paradoxes in their leadership is an indicator that these leaders are leading from the edge" (p. 272).

The comprehensive role of a president has only heightened the complexity already associated with the position (Vaughan and Weisman 1998). Extensive literature on educational administration recognizes a succession of presidents worn down, driven out, or in distress (Hahn 1995). Statistical reports indicate that presidents today serve at a single institution for about 5 to 7 years, representing a much more limited tenure than that of the previous generations of college and university presidents (Basinger 2002). Presidents typically work 55 to 60 hours per week, spending about 22% of their time out of town (Dill 1984, 75). In fact, many would subscribe to the notion that was stated by Rehfuss (1984):

> University presidents have both a difficult and thankless job. They are charged by the trustees to head a balky organization and to correct all previous wrongs. They face a faculty convinced that a president should provide academic leadership (whatever that is) and yet leave well enough alone (not get in the way of the faculty). (P. 64)

Hahn (1995) considers the current pursuit of the presidency as far more serious than ever before and recommends specific criteria for the proper analysis of presidential success. These include longevity, pattern of mobility, and available support system.

According to the *Annual Report of the President's Board on Historically Black Colleges and Universities* (White House Initiative 1999), HBCUs, in addition to ongoing financial difficulties, struggle with changes in many areas such as population demography, technological needs, disadvantaged students, remedial programs and faculty development. Presidents today strive to create a new leadership role that balances HBCU traditions and the new demands being placed upon these institutions in the 21st century.

Community college presidents in many American states are no exception in terms of meeting these same specific demands in higher education. In fact, administrators of community colleges face a unique set of challenges because of the colleges' recent growth trends, in number, size, and complexity of organizational structure. These challenges include the development of a new and enhanced administrative infrastructure, continuing education units, instructional technology, and high turnover among faculty and administrators (Amey, VanDerLinden, and Brown 2002). According to Barwick (2002), the position of the president is very different from other administrative positions in community colleges; therefore, preparation to assume the role of president based on prior academic administrative training is inadequate. In fact, studies indicate that fewer people are applying for community college presidency now than before (Kelley 2002).

In view of these changes and challenges in higher education today, Fincher (1997) suggests that we focus on the importance of the organizational mission, structure, and cultural traditions of colleges and universities as well as individual characteristics of their presidents when measuring leadership effectiveness. According to Fincher, the personal qualities and professional experiences of individual leaders interact with the organizational structure to produce a desired outcome. For example, Birnbaum (1999) emphasizes the understanding of the culture of an institution as a key strategy to assess the leadership effectiveness of a president.

The authors of a series titled *The Presidency* offer suggestions for current and future presidents. Rhodes (1998), a president emeritus, views the academic president as the most influential of all positions. While acknowledging the critical need for successful and innovative leaders during these challenging times, he also considers these times to provide wonderful opportunities for bold and effective leadership.

According to the 2002 Report of the American Council on Education (ACE), most presidents are men and in their late fifties. The average age of presidents is higher today compared to that in 1986; however, the mean age is lower for presidents in liberal arts colleges (Corrigan 2002). The report further indicates that an increasing number of presidents served as administrators and presidents of other colleges and universities before their current positions. It should also be noted that a faculty position is overwhelmingly the entry point for presidents of four-year colleges and universities (Corrigan 2002; Kerr and Gade 1986).

The 2002 report also provides statistics that indicate that a greater percentage of the presidents are married, but the percentage of married presidents is higher among men compared to that among women. The majority, according to the report, hold doctoral degrees. However, research shows that the senior academic administrators of colleges and universities, in addition to their academic qualification and teaching/research experience, need to have certain managerial training in order to move into senior administrative positions in colleges and universities (Cortada 1996; McDade 1988). Peter Drucker (1966) has emphasized that training in management should provide a knowledge base required to deal with the multiple changes associated with the presidency.

A substantial number (about 33%) of college and university presidents move to the position of presidency from the immediate prior position of senior campus executive. However, the highest percentage of female presidents (35%) held a chief academic officer/provost position as their prior administrative position (Corrigan, 2002).

A number of studies on career paths of college CEOs suggest that the most common career progression of a CEO is as follows (in ascending order): faculty, chairperson, dean, vice president for academic affairs/provost and president (Cohen and March 1974; Green 1988; Wessel, and Keim 1994). These authors do not dispute the possibility of a deviation from this traditional track. Along the same line, it is worthwhile to examine the literature on career related issues of women and minority presidents.

Women and Minority Presidents in Higher Education

The study of the state of the college presidency is incomplete without acknowledging the profound influence of race and gender in institutions of higher education (Blake and Moore 1999; Evelyn 1998; Phelps, Tabor, and Smith 1996). Historically, race and gender have played significant roles at all levels of higher education, limiting opportunities for mobility among aspiring administrators (Coleman 1998; Evelyn 1998).

Although the buzzword "diversity" has been around for almost three decades in educational institutions, as well as in corporate America, minority groups (racial and ethnic groups as well as women) continue to be underrepresented in upper tier occupations. According to Shea (2002), women and African Americans hold about 14% and 4% of these high positions, respectively, and 10% of Fortune 500 Board seats. This low minority representation on corporate boards creates limited opportunities to influence issues confronting various institutions of higher education.

The same level of minority representation in America's higher education continues to be a barrier to equal opportunity and career advancement and mobility. The findings of a study by Coleman (1998) on the perception of African American and Caucasian women regarding the effects of race and gender in administrative positions reveal that the most important perceived barriers for these women administrators are racial discrimination, lack of opportunity for upward mobility, and negative attitudes of male administrators. The underrepresentation of women and minorities, particularly in administration, is clearly evident in various research studies (Coleman 1998; Lindsay 1994; Ramey 1995). According to Altbach, Lomotey, and Kyle (1999), administrators in this nation, though concerned, have not placed a high priority on solving their institutions' racial and ethnic problems.

Changes precipitated in the Civil Rights era created an influx of minorities into administrative positions in the 1960s and 1970s. The new pool of minority teachers in the 1960s constituted the future pool of minority administrators (Richards 1988). However, study by the American Council on Education showed that, after excluding HBCUs and Hispanic-Serving Institutions (HSIs), only 10% of colleges and universities are led by minority presidents (Corrigan 2002). The report suggests that colleges and universities have to improve the pipeline of minority faculty and senior staff in order to recruit more minority presidents since the path to presidency begins in the faculty rank.

In a study on college professors and administrators, Rolle, Davis and Banning (2000) found a persistent problem of underrepresentation of African American faculty members at most U.S. colleges and universities. They further observed that the administrators included in the study reported experiencing consistent obstacles to their recruitment, retention, and success. A report based on the compiled statistics in the 2000 issue of the *Journal of Black Issues in Higher Education* (JBHE) supports the above finding by stating that less than two-tenths of one percent of more than 2,100 four-year institutions of higher education in the United States are served by African American presidents (African American presidents 2000). The report further notes that women constitute only 25% of this small fraction of African American presidents.

According to this report, for about two centuries, trustees of colleges and universities were unwilling to even entertain the idea of an African American controlling an institution of higher education. In fact, the JBHE report states that very few African Americans followed in the footsteps of Patrick Francis Healy who in 1874 was the first African American to head a white institution. Today, many African American administrators of higher education have a difficult time imagining that they may be named president of predominantly white colleges and universities. Dr. Ivory Nelson, the president of Central Washington University puts it nicely in a printed piece titled "Unforgettable Presidential Moments" that is published in *Educational Record* (Penney, 1996):

> My two most unforgettable moments were when I was chosen to become the chancellor of Alamo Community College District and later when I was named the president of Central Washington University, both times as the first black president each of these institutions has ever had. When I got that phone call telling me, "You're chosen," it was the American dream for me. The fact that I survived the selection process said something about my skills and qualifications. But, you know, I was surprised. There was only one black person on the board at Alamo, and here at Central Washington there are 169 black stu-

dents out of a total of 8,500 students. I never would have thought it was possible. (P. 23)

Research by JBHE and the *Community College Week* editorial staff reveals that only 5% of the nation's 1,200 two-year institutions are led by African American presidents, of whom about 7% are with HBCUs. JBHE staff attribute this small number to the continued existence of racial stereotypes.

A study by Phelps, Taber, and Smith (1996) reveals that race and gender are influential factors in selecting community college presidents. The study's findings suggest that African American community college presidents are underrepresented in the presidential population despite a slight increase within the last decade. Also evident is that a greater percentage of African American men hold the presidency compared to women (69% male and 31% female). It may be further noted that female presidents in both races are underrepresented.

The difficulties endured by women in rising through the administrative ranks can be attributed to a number of factors. Research has identified several factors that adversely affect women's movement into administration (Ortiz and Marshall 1988). First, values of the society and educational system are least supportive of women aspiring to be administrators. The second factor is a dual track in career paths for men and women, which leads men towards the administrative path and women in the instructional path. Third, the lack of effective "sponsorship" because of the traditional perception of women in instructional roles adversely affects the fulfillment of career aspirations. In fact, sponsorship is very much of a necessity for career mobility of both men and women.

Based on research on women's leadership in educational administration, Gupton and Del Rosario (1997), acknowledged underrepresentation of women in leadership roles as well. However, they identified the areas of concern about women administrators and suggested a shift of focus to these areas to help women advance in their career in an equitable fashion with their male counterparts. These include need for better support systems, appropriate training and education, and a nurturing environment.

It may be noted here, however, that women's roles in higher education have changed a great deal in recent years. Women have made significant progress in holding administrative positions (Rudolph 1990). The number of female presidents doubled between 1986 and 2002. Most of these gains have been in two-year colleges (Kit 2000). Based on the ACE report, Kit acknowledges the increasing diversity among college presidents, but cautions that the rate of advancement is still relatively low.

In addition, inadequate representation of ethnic groups in leadership roles continues to be a matter of concern and debate in higher education (Castenada, Gutierrez, and Katsinas 2002). For instance, although 56% of Hispanics attend community colleges (Hoffman, Snyder, and Sonnenberg 1996), Hispanic presidents in these colleges comprise only about 4% of the total (Vaughan 1996). Hispanic representation in American higher education is disproportionately smaller than Hispanic population growth, which more than doubled nationally between 1980 and 2000 (U.S. Census Bureau 2001). While the researchers of this study acknowledge a small gain in the number of Hispanic doctorates, they also observe that the number of Hispanic administrators holding doctoral degrees is quite modest at best. They further believe that, in aggregate, Hispanics need to enhance their credentials and experience levels in order to achieve higher leadership positions in community colleges. The limited literature on career paths for Hispanics indicates that Hispanics aspiring to and holding faculty and administrative positions continue to be concerned about bias in hiring and promotion policies (Santiago 1996).

The number of Hispanic administrators in higher education increased substantially between 1970s and 1990s, but the number of presidents remained low (Esquibel 1997). Although studies of these administrators are scarce, Esquibel provides some valuable insights based on two comprehensive surveys of Hispanic college presidents conducted in 1976 and 1991. These studies identified factors that are instrumental in enabling Hispanic administrators to move into senior positions. The strong predictors of advancement into senior administrative jobs were educational background, training programs, work experience, and community ties.

Thus, the overall findings reported by Esquibel (1997) suggest that a combination of factors (e.g., personal, professional, demographic, and situational) rather than one single factor tends to influence the career mobility of these senior administrators. These findings mirror the results of a study on the career mobility of upper level Hispanic school administrators (Lopez 1996). The Lopez study suggests that a combination of factors such as gender, personality, experience, and education level predicts the rate of upward mobility among Hispanic administrators.

Kit (2000) reports a growing trend of minority group members holding presidential positions, citing a three percent increase in the number of African American presidents between 1986 and 1998. Kit further notes a similar trend in the hiring of African American presidents (approximately 51) by predominantly white institutions during this same time period. However, African Americans still remain underrepresented in higher level administrative positions in predominantly white colleges and universities. Retention of these administrators on white campuses becomes another challenging and disturbing issue (Jones 2001). While the number of black faculty members has increased at two-year and four-year institutions, only 156 African American administrators hold the positions of president or provost (Wilson 1996).

Literature on African American women as administrators in higher education is also scarce. As Chamberlain (1988) said,

> Women of color are rarely recognized as having unique needs. Therefore, separate studies and data are seldom available on minority women, especially by racial and ethnic group. This may be caused by the small representation in higher education. (P. 114)

During the 1980s, African American female administrators were simultaneously perceived as an endangered species in white academia and as simply tokens in higher education (Mosley 1980). During the 1990s, only a handful of African American women were appointed college presidents, in direct contrast to the public positioning of educational institutions as equal opportunity, affirmative action employers that emphasized their strong interest in minority groups and women applying for such positions (Lindsay 1994).

According to Lomotey (1997), female African American leaders are in scarce supply in managerial positions as well as in senior positions in higher education. In his book, *Sailing against the Wind*, he explained how the career mobility of African American women is limited because they are consistently ignored for promotions in spite of their educational and experiential credentials. He further notes that white women who pursue higher education while in clerical jobs are considered more favorably for promotion compared with African American women who are already knowledgeable and experienced in the relevant areas of work and study.

Statistics on African American faculty members and administrators in Alabama's traditional white institutions between 1989 and 1997 indicate very little improvement in African American presence (Evelyn 1998). African Americans continue to represent only two percent to eight percent of the total population of these institutions. Additionally, retention of black students, faculties, and administrators on white campuses seems to be an ongoing challenge (Jones 2001). A number of studies indicate evidence of racial inequality and negative stereotypes against minorities in white colleges and universities (Bennefield 1999; Harvey 1999). These studies reveal serious concerns about the existing inequality in resources and offer suggestions for its remedy. Several studies indicate race as a critical factor in every aspect of the administrative career (Rolley 2000). Jones (2001) conducted a survey of literature about African American college and university administrators and provided an understanding of the pathways and barriers to success. He notes that these administrators consider community support and mentoring to be very important for overcoming existing barriers.

African Americans remain underrepresented in high level administrative jobs in white colleges and universities. Between 1970 and 2000, 52 of 2,100 traditional white institutions had African American presidents. Only 14 of these 52 presidents were black females (Adams 2001). Currently, only 63 African Americans hold the position of president or chancellor at two-year colleges (Evelyn 1998).

According to the American Council on Education (Ross and Green 1998), the number of female presidents has doubled within the last five years, while the percentage of minority presidents has increased by only three percent. However, women's gains in academia and other professions have not been evenly distributed across all types of organizations (Warner and Defleur 1993). The gains are even fewer for minority women (Ross and Green 1998), further validating the "glass ceiling" phenomenon, which remains firmly embedded in our society (Mason 1993).

Institutions for higher education hold great symbolic value in society since, "in their daily institutional practices . . . they can either recreate anew the ideals of democracy or perpetuate the gulf of despair built on caste and class" (Richards 1988, 160). Craig Richards, in *The Search for Equity in Educational Administration*, remarks on the significance of improving minority representation in colleges:

> These positions are highly visible; they signal institutional commitment to equity for all other units within the organization. Furthermore, when women and minorities secure highly visible leadership positions in educational institutions, the organization signals the legitimacy of affirmative action and equal opportunity to the wider society, diminishes the power of stereotypes, provides role models for children and young adults, and confirms experientially the democratic ideals taught in the classroom. (P. 160)

In recognition of this need to combat pervasive obstacles and barriers based on race and gender, both African American and white institutions have attempted to create opportunities for change in order to diversify the upper echelons of higher education. For example, historically black colleges and universities, which have provided low-income black students access to higher education, have developed new strategies of student recruitment and new partnerships with white colleges (Sims 1994). Predominantly white universities have introduced programs and curriculum changes to motivate and retain African American students and administrators on their campuses. Nevertheless, these institutions have not achieved a high degree of success in this area. In fact, a new type of segregation is appearing in some prestigious educational institutions that have designed attractive programs to increase the number of African Americans on their campuses (Blake and Moore 1999).

Undoubtedly, the glass ceiling that is defined as an unseen force against career advancement is very real and affects equal access by women and minorities to higher education (Vander Woerdt 1992). The glass ceiling, according to Vander Woerdt, prevents minorities from exploring their potential equally in various administrative positions. This may reasonably explain the lack of adequate representation of female and African American administrators (Coleman 1998). Coleman's study further reveals that most African American and white female administrators perceive racial discrimination, negative attitudes toward women and inadequate opportunities for upward mobility as barriers to their career progression. However, a qualitative study by Lindsey (1994), based on in-depth interviews with three minority female administrators, suggested another perspective on race and gender issues. She found that, although her subjects acknowledged the "Good Old Boy network" as a factor in career progression, they perceived their gender and race as positive features of their administrative effectiveness, enabling them to establish trust, communication, and nurturing relationships with minority and international colleagues and students.

At this point, it is useful to examine the available literature on issues confronting administrative leaders in historically black colleges and universities.

Historically Black Colleges and Universities

Historical Overview

According to a report published in the White House Initiative on Historically Black Colleges and Universities (1997), the Higher Education Act of 1965, as amended, defines an HBCU as follows:

> Any historically black college or university that was established prior to 1964, whose principal mission was and is the education of black Americans and that is accredited by a nationally recognized accrediting agency or association determined by the Secretary (of Education) to be a reliable authority as to the quality of training offered or is according to such an agency or association making reasonable progress toward accreditation. (P. 7)

According to the National Center for Education Statistics (Hoffman, Snyder, and Sonnenberg 1996), there are 103 HBCUs, consisting of 53 private and 50 public institutions. These include 89 four-year and 14 two-year colleges. Most HBCUs are located in Southern states. The geography, type, size, and curricula at HBCUs are as diverse as that of white universities (Gray 1997). For example, HBCUs represent a wide spectrum of institutional variations, including single-sex, coeducational, church-related, secular, research-oriented, liberal arts, small, large, undergraduate-only, and graduate-level institutions (Gray 1997). Data provided by NAFEO Research Institute (Myers and Roscoe 1994) indicate that by 1993, there were 15 HBCUs that granted doctorates, 39 HBCUs that offered master's degrees, and 85 HBCUs that provided bachelor's degrees.

Historically black colleges and universities have played a critical role in higher education by providing opportunities for a large number of African Americans (Gray 1997). William Gray III, President of the United Negro College Fund (UNCF), noted that about 8000 HBCU graduates served in various capacities in World War II. HBCUs are certainly a major part of mainstream American higher education today (Richmond and Maramark 1996). Research suggests that despite unique challenges, an increasing number of HBCUs, through business and continuing education departments, are contributing to the economic development of their respective communities, regions, and states.

The recent establishment of the White House Initiative on HBCUs (1997) under the Clinton Administration, as a vehicle to strengthen HBCUs, reaffirms their continuing importance in higher education today.

Lincoln University, the first institution founded by the Presbyterian Church in Pennsylvania in 1854, and Wilberforce University, founded by the African Methodist Episcopal Church in Ohio in 1856, were the first two institutions established on the eve of the Civil War to provide opportunities to African Americans seeking a college education (Williams 1988). Thompson (1973) states that these colleges served as the only reliable opportunities for African American youth to receive a higher level of education. Prior to these institutions, access to higher education was limited to the economic elite only.

Williams (1988) observed that the majority of HBCUs were founded after the Civil War. The establishment of HBCUs was based on the belief that African Americans who were free after the Civil War should be educated. Under the auspices of Congressional legislation known as the First and Second Morril Acts of 1862 and 1882, public land-grant colleges were established to provide higher education to less wealthy Americans. Black institutions and white institutions were established as a result of these Acts.

Many segments of society played major roles in the establishment of HBCUs (Smith 1981). The 1995 issue of *Academe* reports that between 1865 and 1875, 24 black colleges were founded and supported by certain states and church groups. These colleges became instrumental in African American participation in higher education, particularly since state sponsored segregation laws denied African Americans entrance into white universities (Smith 1981).

The original HBCUs faced obstacles such as conflicting perspectives on the kind of education that should be offered. The debate was articulated most cogently by two well known educators, Booker T. Washington and W.E.B. DuBois. However, differences in vision did not prevent these institutions from growing (Garibaldi 1984). Although the debates between these great educators have become historically significant, they never deterred the ability of African American colleges to enjoy success in society. Whiting (1991) succinctly explains,

> Therefore, the historic mission of minority institutions should not be their only reason for being. It is too self-limiting, too comfortable operationally, and risks numbing inertia and competitive disadvantage. . . .There is no single prescription for the future. But it is clear that an adamant retention of an official emphasis on "Blackness" and confinement to the psychology of the minority community as opposed to "mainstreaming" will not serve these institutions or their students very well in the future. (P. 71).

Historically black colleges and universities continue to play an integral part in our nation's educational system today in the face of new challenges like increasing costs, accreditation pressures, declining enrollment, and competition from predominantly white institutions (Turner 2002). For example, HBCUs have reportedly achieved a significant level of success in terms of racial integration and diversity among students, faculties, and administrators (Gray 1997). Based on statistics reported by Gray, about 11% of students in HBCUs are white compared to only 6% of students at other colleges who are African American. The report further indicates that about 20% of faculty and 10% of administrators at HBCUs are white, while only 2% of faculty and 1.5% of administrators at other colleges are African American.

Beverly Lindsey (1994), a senior administrator of Hampton University and an administrator with experience at both predominantly white and black colleges, comments:

> I was one of the first to experience "integration" in the immediate wake of *Brown v. Board of Education of Topeka, Kansas* (1954). Now, 40 years later, I am a dean at a historically black university, after spending nearly 15 years in administrative and faculty positions at predominantly European American universities. As I reflect on my experiences in both types of higher educational settings, I clearly recognize that *Brown* has not achieved what many optimistic and progressive African Americans and other Americans had envisioned, particularly for African American women as administrators in higher education. (P. 430)

Role of HBCUs

HBCUs have trained African Americans to face America's economic, social, and political challenges for the past 150 years. Many have advanced the belief that these institutions possess the unique capability of addressing African American needs and transforming students of inadequate secondary education into talented and contributing citizens. In fact, a significant number of college presidents have received bachelor's degrees from HBCUs (Roach 2000).

William H. Gray III (1997) states that 45% of recent African American Ph.D.s received their undergraduate degrees at HBCUs, and that more than one-half of all African-American professionals are graduates of HBCUs. He believes that young African Americans will increasingly be drawn to HBCUs where they can find role models and a non-hostile and nurturing environment. He further states:

> Since 1835, these colleges and universities have persevered through difficult and challenging times to prepare leaders for America. Just as the religious and ethnic colleges of early immigrants—Georgetown, Yeshiva, Brigham Young—provided doorways for their rejected communities, HBCUs continue to serve all of us. They have a vital role to play. From their halls have come—and will continue to come—the business persons, physicians, scientists, engineers, architects, teachers, public servants, and artists we need to be strong in the twenty-first century. (Par. 3)

In spite of a decline in student enrollment in HBCUs due to increased educational opportunities in predominantly white institutions after 1950, statistical reports consistently show higher graduation rates in HBCUs (Hoffman, Snyder, and Sonnenberg 1996). This study, published by the National Center for Educational Statistics, reports that HBCUs represent only three percent of all the nation's institutions of higher education in the United States, but produce one third of all African American college graduates. In addition, HBCUs have opened their doors to students regardless of race, creed, gender, or national origin (Allen and Jewell 2002).

According to Lockett (1994), HBCUs have contributed to the knowledge of their students' professions and have taught them the art of practicing these professions in the mainstream. He further reports that HBCUs may hold the key to empowering students by developing their full potential and cultivating community leaders and thinkers.

A study across nine HBCUs and 91 non-HBCUs, conducted by McClure, Rao, and Lester (1999), which compared students in terms of their attitudes toward general education and personal growth, revealed that students attending HBCUs tend to have more positive perceptions about their general education and personal growth compared to non-HBCU students. HBCU students also rated higher in personal growth with respect to political awareness and personal value factors.

Although HBCUs are at a crossroads, facing increasingly diverse challenges in the 21st century, they are viable institutions with unique abilities to empower, encourage, and enrich the lives of young African Americans (Henderson 2001; Turner 2002). According to the 1971 Carnegie Commission on Higher Education report, as cited in *Black Issues in Higher Education* (African American presidents 2000),

> HBCUs assumed leadership for the Black community; stimulated the interest of Black youth in higher education; served as custodians for the archives of African Americans; developed learning methodologies for overcoming handicaps of the educationally disadvantaged; developed and expanded programs for educating and retraining Black adults; and provided educational opportunities for students who fall short of admission requirements of conventional institutions of higher education. (P. 50)

The enrollment of African American students at HBCUs has reached an all-time high of 360,000 students, an increase of 26% over the past 18 years (Henderson 2001). A recent report issued by the American Association of University Professors (AAUP) provided scholarly evidence in support of preserving HBCUs and countered the threat by some state and federal government officials to make attendance at HBCUs optional (Hawkins 1995). This action reaffirms AAUP support for the preservation of the unique role of HBCUs.

However, like all institutions of higher education, HBCUs need quality leadership to face current and future challenges. In fact, a new generation of presidents has now emerged, possessing unique skills and training to lead these institutions using new and creative approaches (New black college presidents 1999). These presidents are committed to a broad vision, goals, and leadership style, while valuing the traditions of HBCUs. Presidents with administrative experiences in predominantly white institutions and professional experience at HBCUs are making deliberate choices to serve HBCUs. An overview of HBCU presidents based on available literature will provide a better understanding of these leaders.

Presidents

African American college presidents that lead HBCUs must undertake multiple roles in shaping the direction of higher education in the United States. They must possess certain leadership characteristics, both personal and professional, in order to meet the challenges. They are expected to be capable of implementing many programs and policies while generating funds to support and sustain these institutions.

As Cunningham (1992) emphasizes, HBCU administrators must have increased training in various facets of institutional leadership. According to the National Association for Equal Opportunity (NAFEO) Research Institute (Myers and Roscoe 1994), the current presidents/chancellors are also the chief administrative officers of HBCUs. The goal of the leader is not only to survive, but also to set a new direction in higher education.

From a demographics perspective, about 85% of the 103 HBCU presidents are men (Corrigan 2002). African American Presidents head most HBCUs (96%). A significant number of presidents are married and are in their late 50s during their tenure. Most presidents had held faculty positions for a number of years. Their major field of study has typically been Education. Female presidents lead about 75% of women's colleges.

The early presidents, through the 1960s, were strong administrators. They were politically and managerially sophisticated. Leadership continued to change in the 1970s and 1980s as desegregation increased.

The modern HBCU president is expected to play a demanding role in the educational community (Whiting 1991). *Ebony* (New black college presidents 1999, par. 6) quotes Carlton E. Brown, president of Savannah State University: "The new leader needs to be broadly knowledgeable, have a strong grasp of finance, technology and teamwork, and needs to be a perpetual change agent." It is therefore worthwhile to examine the factors that determine the upward professional mobility of persons who are selected for this demanding leadership position. A conceptual and theoretical framework on professional mobility as addressed in literature should be examined.

Conceptual/Theoretical Framework: Career Mobility and Internal Labor Markets

Upward professional mobility for this study is defined as career progression in the hierarchy of administration in academia. There are many theories pertaining to career mobility in institutions of higher education (Vardi 1980). The basic framework of career mobility is grounded in occupational sociology, labor sociology, labor economics, and organizational phenomena. Although no particular theory aligns perfectly with the administrative career mobility of HBCU presidents, the theoretical framework for this study is grounded in the concept of career mobility and internal labor market theory.

Career Mobility

Careers are complex by nature and they provide a major source of identity for working individuals. Hall (1976) views careers as a progression of occupations resulting in an increase in status, prestige, skill and attitude. According to Wilensky (1960), a career is "a succession of related jobs, arranged in hierarchy of prestige" through which persons move in more or less predictable sequences. Twombly (1986a) defines careers as "structures of organizations through which the process of recruiting, training, socializing, and allocating the right individuals to the right positions at the right time takes place" (p. 3). These viewpoints characterize a career as an enhanced movement for gaining knowledge and skills to allow for further advancement.

Glaser (1968) identifies the function of career as follows:

> In general, organizations obtain work from people by offering them some kind of career within their structures. The operation of organizations, therefore, depends on people's assuming a career orientation toward them. To generate this orientation, organizations distribute rewards, working conditions, and prestige to their members according to career level; thus these benefits are properties of their organizational careers. (P. 1)

A career in organizations like colleges and universities typically begins with a teaching position. An individual may remain in a teaching position throughout his or her career or may move to an administrative position (Twombly 1986). A career in administration may encompass a series of jobs involving the tasks of management that tend to have increasing responsibility.

Career mobility is the movement from one position to another (Thompson, Avery, and Carlson 1968). Although career mobility implies upward movement through a hierarchy of positions, movement may also be lateral or even downward (Vardi 1980). For example, Ross and Green (1998) found that 20% of college presidents had been presidents of other institutions.

The career patterns of administrators are not as clearly structured as those of faculty in higher education (Twombly 1986a). Cohen and March (1974) proposed the normative career ladder that was comprised of sequential administrative positions—from faculty to president. However, a study conducted by Moore (1983) to evaluate presidents, provosts, and deans through the normative ladder indicated no single dominant career path to the presidency. The majority of presidents had skipped several rungs on the career ladder. However, the career ladder described by Cohen and March (1974) is probably applicable and accurate with certain variations incorporated (Moore, Salambene, and Bragg 1983). This study reported that the identification of the entry port for administrators into academia is accurate and useful. Most positions that presidents held fell into the typical administrative career path. For example, African American presidents had held many administrative positions prior to the current presidency, but not in a sequential basis (Corrigan 2002). The report further notes that most presidents enter higher education through faculty positions. In essence, the normative career ladder is simply a general guide to explain career paths.

According to Twombly (1986a), an examination of mobility within organizations is required to assess individual professional outcomes as functions of individual characteristics as well as work structures. Twombly used models that focus on individuals as well as organizational structures.

The individual level of analysis targets factors based on psychological and sociological concepts. Psychological concepts generally include personality, satisfaction, and aspiration. Sociological concepts tend to include career patterns, life stages, individual characteristics, and career behavior (Vardi 1980). A number of studies place attention on the demographic characteristics of those who hold a particular office. Perhaps the American Council on Education reports (i.e., Corrigan 2002; Ross and Green 1998), based on a national survey of presidents of colleges and universities including HBCUs, is the most well known example of this type of study.

A number of studies examining the administrative career of presidents and other administrators within higher education have demonstrated that the mobility of administrators is influenced by structural variables such as region, affiliation, size, institutional type, resource level, prior position, and administrative specialties (Smolansky 1984; Twombly 1986a). Researchers have also identified sponsorship as a key variable (potentially structural) that wields significant influence in career mobility (Valverde and Brown 1988). Valverde and Brown observe,

> Prevailing sentiment has long supported the view that advancement into administrative ranks is competitive, encompassing formal preparation and state certification. Alongside a pattern of school administration based on preparation and merit has grown a system of sponsorship by university faculty and organizational superiors that some observers believe more significantly influences promotion than open competition. (P. 151)

In a study of professional mobility, Birnbaum (1970) discovered that very few university presidents moved across institutional types. For example, most presidents in two-year colleges continue to move within two-year institutions rather than transition to four-year colleges. He noted that a pool of viable candidates for an institution's presidency is populated primarily from similar institutions with a similar student admission policy and mission rather than from institutions of different sizes. Through their research, Ross and Green (1990) confirmed the lack of mobility across institutional types. According to Smolansky (1984), inter-institutional mobility usually occurs among institutions of the same type.

Hall (1976) considered a need for the integration of individual and organizational factors. Vardi (1980) developed a model of the combination of both factors where the mobility rates are used as dependent variables and individual characteristics are used as predictors. Applications of this model seem relevant since HBCUs are institutions that are unique in the mission of providing a quality education to African Americans (Allen and Jewell 2002). While the mission, policies, and programs of HBCUs are being revisited and refined to introduce appropriate changes, their boards and administrators are committed to maintaining institutional traditions (Henderson 2001).

Internal Labor Market Theory

The concept of internal labor market was defined by Dunlop (1966) as "the complex of rules which determine the movement of workers among job classifications within administrative units, such as enterprises, companies, or hiring halls" (p. 32). Moore, Martorana, and Twombley (1985) defined the concept further by characterizing internal labor markets as organizational structures, through which workers moved from low-level entry positions upward through the organizational hierarchy. The concept has evolved in other ways, as researchers have applied it to various occupations and careers, and has expanded beyond the "administrative unit" envisioned by Dunlop. Specifically, Althauser and Kalleberg (1981) made a distinction between "firm internal labor markets" which were confined to a single employer, and "occupational internal labor markets," which grouped related occupations spanning more than one employer.

Several studies have linked the concept of the occupational internal labor market to career mobility in higher education. Twombley (1988) observed that academic careers do not exist solely at a single institution. Ross and Green (1998) reported that 68% of all presidents are recruited from the same type of institution. Smolansky (1984) identified the occupational internal labor market as inclusive of several educational institutional types in her study of job transition behavior of administrators in higher education. Thus the identification of careers within higher education as falling within the concept of internal labor market theory is well documented.

Internal labor markets include three structural features: (a) they require employees to begin in lower-level entry ports; (b) they develop job ladders to minimize cost; and (c) the movement up the job ladder is associated with a progressive development of knowledge and skill (Bills 1987; Althauser and Kalleberg 1981). In essence, in order for an internal market to exist, there must be a mobility chain, entry positions, and education occurring in the process of career advancement (Althauser and Kallenberg 1981). The basic assumption of this theory is that, over a period of time, institutions develop a sequence of positions that afford opportunities to employees to climb up the ladder within an institution or across similar institutions. Furthermore, these higher positions are assumed to entail greater responsibilities compared to lower positions.

One variation of this theory, the institutionally segmented labor-market model, supports the idea that in larger internal markets, career advancement may be more a function of administrative rules and procedures, than pure supply and demand (Boyan 1988, 163). In addressing the underrepresentation of minorities in higher education, this particular version argues that "rules and procedures (e.g. seniority) were collusive in that they protected the jobs of white males at the expense of women and minorities" (Boyan 1988, 163).

Data collected by the American Council on Education (Corrigan 2002) and other studies clearly reveal that a greater percent of HBCU presidents begin their career in faculty positions and move to other institutions to assume higher positions, but not necessarily in sequence. HBCU presidents, according to this report, hold many senior level executive positions (e.g. vice-president and provost) before becoming president. Of course, there is an increasing trend of presidents moving to other institutions in the same position. This probably will further introduce a new dimension to the career patterns of presidents.

Currently few studies exist on administrative career mobility in higher education from a structural perspective, and none of these studies is directed specifically at HBCUs. Yet the data available, including those dealing with the entry ports of HBCU presidents, their educational and experiential advancement through upward movement in position, and their prior administrative positions within other institutions of the same types, seem to be consistent with the criteria of the internal labor market theory.

Chapter 3

Methodology

The introductory chapter of this study outlined the limited research on professional mobility as it pertains to administrative careers of African American college and university presidents. There is certainly a dearth of literature and studies on African American presidents of historically black colleges and universities in this regard. The absence of consistent research efforts relative to the administrative careers of these chief executive officers in higher education has resulted in a void in systematic gathering of information in this area. One major source of information and statistics on college and university presidents, the American Council of Education (ACE) reports (i.e., Corrigan, 2002; Ross and Green, 1998), however, has emerged in recent years. The ACE, which developed a report on the profile of college presidents in 1986, annually updates the database on these presidents and has published reports on a regular basis. However, most research in career related fields pertaining to senior level administrators of colleges and universities, particularly African American presidents, has utilized qualitative data and to a limited extent survey data in their methodology.

This chapter describes the methodological strategy, which takes a quantitative approach and includes a qualitative component as well. The methodology is designed primarily to identify and examine the relationship between HBCU presidents' rates of upward professional mobility and selected biographical predictors in the demographic, social, educational, occupational, and organizational areas, based on unobtrusive biographical data. It is also designed to (a) identify common traits and characteristics of African American presidents of HBCUs associated with their upward professional mobility; (b) compare African American presidents of HBCUs and those of the traditionally white universities in terms of specific traits and characteristics affecting their upward mobility; and (c) explore specific trend and career patterns of these presidents, if any such patterns emerge from the data.

The chapter is divided into four sections: (a) Research Design; (b) Participants; (c) Materials, and (d) Procedures.

Research Design

The research design of this study is a combination of quantitative and qualitative type designs. The quantitative research design used is the causal comparative design, which is used when a researcher wants to find out the cause of a phenomenon (rate of mobility) that has already occurred and which cannot be easily examined through experimental means. The qualitative design used is the grounded theory, which allows the researcher to come up with an abstract explanation or understanding of a process based on information from the study.

The information gathered on several biographical traits and characteristics of the African American presidents of HBCUs served as independent variables and the rate of upward professional mobility of African American presidents of HBCUs was the dependent variable. The biographical variables (the independent variables) in this study were selected from various trajectories, such as personal, demographic, educational, career, and organizational attributes. They include gender, educational background variables (type of institution attended, additional studies/training, area of specialization), region of birth, faculty experience, and work experience at HBCUs.

Other variables indicating specific traits and characteristics that are associated with presidents' upward professional mobility were also examined to answer specific research questions designed in this study. They include current age, age at presidency, marital status, level of education, type of degree obtained, highest degree earned, work experience, position prior to presidency, African American organizational affiliation.

As mentioned earlier, upward professional mobility for this study was defined as the rate of career progression in the administrative career of the African American presidents (see table 3.1).

Table 3.1 *Definitions of different mobility rates*

Mobility rate	Years of progression to presidency (years)
High	7-12
Moderate	13-18
Low	19 and above

Participants

The population of this study consisted of 103 African Americans identified as chief executive officers (CEOs, presidents, or chancellors) of historically black colleges and universities throughout the United States. The sample, however, consisted of the number of presidents for whom complete biographical data were available. According to the *Higher Education Directory* (Torregrosa, 2002), HBCU presidents are located in 14 Southern states, 6 Northern states, 3 midwestern states, the District of Columbia, and the Virgin Islands. In this study, African American presidents serving HBCUs as of January 2003 are included. The selection of the presidents was based on the availability of comprehensive biographical information. The sample size of 72 participants obtained was more than 70% of the population of 103. In addition, data on 22 African American university presidents of non-HBCUs were collected, analyzed, and compared to data obtained on African American HBCU presidents.

Materials

This study utilized unobtrusive measures based upon biographical data about African American presidents of HBCUs. Literature suggests many uses and advantages of unobtrusive measures. Sechrest (1980) defines unobtrusive measures as non-reactive methods of gathering data: that is, means of obtaining information in which subjects are not aware of being studied. Adler and Clark (1999) describe unobtrusive measures as indicators of interactions, events, or behaviors under consideration which do not affect the data collected even if the original collection of data may not have been unobtrusive. They further state that the use of these available data rules out the possibility of the research findings being affected by the process of data collection, unlike survey, observations, and experiments. According to Steward (1984), the use of unobtrusive research means resourceful use of the mountains of data generated to address research questions across various disciplines. It is also stated that unobtrusive study involves strategies that are quite interesting and innovative for the collection and assessment of data (Berg 2001). In fact, Berg suggests several ways researchers can practice using unobtrusive measures, one of which is the use of biographical data, particularly if data are readily accessible.

The validity and reliability of readily accessible data may be achieved in several ways. According to Babbie (2001), validity refers to the degree to which a criterion actually measures the characteristics or phenomena it claims to measure and reliability depends on the consistency of the outcome if the same instrument is used. Assessment of validity and reliability in unobtrusive biographical data depends mostly on the credibility and integrity of the sources that collect and compile these data. The National Association for Equal Opportunity (NAFEO), one of the HBCU representative associations founded in 1969, promotes activities that have influenced national and international appreciation for the attributes of the HBCUs (National Association 2002). NAFEO represents all HBCUs—public, private, two-year, and four-year institutions and is considered to play a pivotal future role in strengthening the HBCUs (Thomas and Green 1993). NAFEO's commitment to collect and compile pertinent data on the HBCUs and their presidents is evident from its use as a reference source in a number of studies (Elam 1989; Myers and Roscoe 1994; Sutton 1994).

The United Negro College Fund (UNCF), another HBCU representative association and fundraising organization for its member HBCUs, has established its credibility by the contributions it has made to strengthening these institutions academically. It has also taken a firm stand on the continuing need for HBCUs (Roebuck and Murty 1993). The UNCF's newsletter, *The University Faculty Voice*, and its use as references in various studies (Roebuck and Murty 1993;

Wilson, 1990) provide evidence of the organization's seriousness in producing quality data.

Although, based on the researcher's knowledge, *Who's Who among African Americans* (Bennett et al. 2001) has not been used in studies pertaining to administrators in higher education, the data should be regarded as valid and reliable because they are provided to the publishers of *Who's Who among African Americans* by the subjects themselves, through responses to a questionnaire sent out by the publishers. The subjects are top level administrators who are highly visible publicly themselves and who have a personal stake in providing honest and accurate information. The information they provided for publication is subject not only to public view but also to the view of their peers and colleagues. According to Berg (2001), public archival data recorded in books, magazines, and newspapers are viewed as typically prepared for the expressed purpose of examination by others. Furthermore, the data published in these annual directories are individualized, not aggregated, and therefore are subjected to less error.

Thus, familiarity with the information, understanding of the content, and answering of the questions may be ways to enhance the validity and reliability of the instrument. Because this study deals with biographical data that are fact-based and structured, the problems of reliability and validity inherent in data recording attitudes and opinions are greatly minimized.

Who's Who among African Americans, previously named *Who's Who among Black Americans*, has been around for about twenty years, indicating its high credibility as a data source. This is a public document that is widely available, and is found in most public and institutional libraries throughout the country. This directory lists over twenty thousand men and women who are notable African Americans, and it contains comprehensive biographical information about them. Finally, for verification purpose, a sample of the data reported in *Who's Who among African Americans* was tested by comparing it with the biographical data for the same individuals reported in NAFEO (NAFEO profile 2002, Quick reference 1998) and consistency was found. This indicates that *Who's Who among African Americans* has criterion validity.

Procedures

Data were collected from a variety of sources by the researcher and appropriately tabulated. The main sources of data collection for this study were NAFEO (National Association 2002), which provides profile data of African American HBCU presidents; *Who's Who among African Americans*, 14th (Bennett et al. 2001) and 15th (Henderson and York 2002) editions, and *Who's Who in America* (2002), which list biographical information by various dimensions: personal, demographic, career, organizational, and honors/awards; UNCF publications, and Internet websites, which are used to obtain information on the current presidents serving HBCUs.

The list of HBCUs and their presidents was obtained from NAFEO and UNCF (NAFEO profile 2002, Quick reference 1998, United Negro College

Fund 2002). These organizations often compile this type of information during their annual membership drives. This information was verified by the *Higher Education Directory* (Torregrosa 2002). NAFEO data and data in *Who's Who among African Americans* were used to obtain information on HCBU presidents' personal, demographic, social, educational, and career-related traits and characteristics. While data provided in NAFEO are detailed and comprehensive, *Who's Who among African Americans* serves to complement NAFEO in providing complete biographical information on these presidents. The *Chronicle of Higher Education*, the *University Faculty Voice* published by UNCF, and various websites that provide information on African American presidents were used for supplementary data as appropriate. As indicated earlier, African American presidents with substantially available biographical data constituted the sample for this study.

Data for each president was recorded according to the list of variables identified as independent and dependent variables. The attributes of these variables that were found pertinent to this study were coded numerically and then inputted to a codebook to prepare for data entry and analysis. Data cleaning techniques were used to assure quality. Data cleaning involves a process that detects and corrects coding errors (Babbie 2001). Babbie recommends data cleaning because errors in coding are common and inevitable, regardless of the method of data entry.

Data for this research study were analyzed through the use of a computer database using Statistical Packages for the Social Sciences (SPSS) software. The quantitative elements of data analysis included descriptive statistics, cross-tabulations, and chi-square test.

Descriptive statistics present data quantitatively in a manageable form and are used to describe single variables as well as associations between two variables (Babbie 2001). According to Heiman (2000), descriptive statistics are specific procedures for describing the important characteristics of a sample. In this study, descriptive statistics such as percentage and frequency distributions were used to identify and explain specific traits and characteristics of African American presidents of HBCUs and traditionally white universities, specifically as they relate to upward mobility in the presidents' administrative careers. Descriptive analysis also forms the basis of qualitative research with regard to trends and patterns that may emerge.

Cross tabulations and chi-square tests were also used to examine the varying rate of upward mobility based on certain biographical predictors since these variables were mostly categorical. According to Babbie (2001), cross tabulation and chi-square tests are used for variables that are categorical and are measured at either nominal or ordinal level. Chi-square is also used as a test of significance, based on the null hypothesis that there is no relationship or difference between two variables in the population (Ritchey 2000).

The qualitative aspects of the study explored specific trends or patterns pertaining to the data on African American presidents. Data analysis for this part was based on the finding of these patterns during the course of the study.

Chapter 4

Analysis of Data

Public archival sources, as described in Chapter 3, yielded biographical data on 72 African American presidents of historically black colleges and universities (HBCUs) and 22 African American presidents of traditionally white institutions (TWIs). These data were subjected to statistical analysis using the computer program SPSS, in order to explore the rates and patterns of mobility of African American college and university presidents.

This chapter presents the results of the analysis, organized in terms of the seven research questions outlined in Chapter 1. The analyses include (1) the demographic, educational, and career profile of the sample of interest; (2) educational disciplines; (3) gender-based differences; (4) additional professional training; (5) marital status, age, and state of origin; (6) entry position; and (7) differences between African American presidents of HBCUs and or traditionally white institutions. Each research question is addressed for the analysis of data collected and in terms of its findings. In addition, a few ancillary findings are presented.

Analysis of data for this study is based on descriptive statistics and cross tabulation with chi-square tests, as appropriate, to answer specific research questions. Descriptive statistics were used mostly to address the pattern of upward mobility by identifying and analyzing common characteristics along demographic, educational, and career dimensions. Cross tabulation analysis and chi-square tests for statistical significance were performed to examine the relationship between rates of mobility and the variables representing certain individual characteristics.

Research Questions

Research Question 1

Are there commonalities in specific demographic, educational, and career profiles of African American presidents in historically black colleges and universities? If so, what are they?

This research question pertains to data on demographic variables such as current age, age at presidency, gender, state of origin, and marital status; educational variables, such as degrees earned at the undergraduate and graduate level, types of institutions attended for these degrees, and the academic discipline; and variables in areas of career related characteristics, experiences and positions held at HBCUs as well as non HBCUs. Tables 4.1, 4.2, and 4.3 present summaries of results on these variables through descriptive statistics.

Table 4.1 *Demographic profile of African American presidents of HBCUs*

Characteristics	Frequency	Percentage
Current Age		
40-49	3	4.17
50-59	32	44.44
60-69	25	34.72
70-79	11	15.28
Not available	1	1.39
Total	72	100.00
Age at Presidency		
30-39	8	11.11
40-49	29	40.28
50-59	30	41.67
60-69	3	4.17
Not available	2	2.77
Total	72	100.00
Gender		
Female	16	22.22
Male	56	77.78
Total	72	100.00
Birth Region		
West	6	8.33
South	32	44.44
East	2	2.78
Midwest	13	18.06
North	13	18.06
Not available	6	8.33
Total	72	100.00
Marital Status		
Married	55	76.39
Divorced	5	6.94
Not reported	12	16.67
Total	72	100.00

Table 4.1 shows that the most common age range of African Americans who are currently serving as presidents of HBCUs is between the ages of 50 to 69. However, 82% of presidents assumed presidency between ages 40 and 59. The percentage of African Americans assuming presidency is about the same in age categories 40-49 and 50-59. Three-quarters of the participants were male.

Most (44.4%) were born in the South. About 18% were born in the Midwest and the same percentage were born in the North. Data in Table 4.2 show that about 76% of African American presidents of HBCUs are married. The pattern in the demographic profile of African American presidents of HBCUs who have attained the highest position in their career hierarchy in colleges and universities clearly reflects that most presidents are men from the Southern part of the United States who are between 50-69 years of age, and are married.

Table 4.2 shows the educational profile of African American presidents of HBCUs. Most (about 66%) earned their undergraduate degrees from HBCUs. However, the ratio changes at the master's degree level, in that more than half received their masters degree from non-HBCUs. Almost 90% of African American presidents received their doctoral degree from universities other than HBCUs compared to about 10% obtaining the degree from HBCUs. This low percentage may be because very few HBCUs offer doctoral degrees. A small percentage (about 10-12%) of these presidents received their masters or doctoral degrees from Ivy League schools. Data also suggest that a majority of these presidents—about 61%—hold a Ph.D. and only about 21% hold an Ed.D. as their terminal degrees. The average number of years between the receipt of the bachelors and masters degree for presidents was about 4 years. The average number of years these presidents waited after the masters degree to receive the doctoral degree was about 11 years. A slightly greater percentage of presidents (about 57% and 47%) completed bachelors and masters degrees in liberal arts rather than natural science and mathematics. The major area of study for the doctoral degree for the majority of presidents is education (41%). The next most popular disciplines are social sciences and natural sciences. A few listed business or other disciplines as their fields of study. Both male and female presidents show a similar pattern in their academic disciplines.

In summary, the data show that the president of an HBCU is likely to have received his or her undergraduate degree at an HBCU, but the masters and terminal degree at a non-HBCU. He or she is likely to have majored in education as the academic discipline, and is slightly more likely to have received a BA and MA rather than a BS and MS degree.

Table 4.3 presents certain career related characteristics of African American presidents of HBCUs. About half received additional training after the terminal degree. This training usually consisted of post-doctoral studies or research, or further professional development through management related courses. More than 50% entered their careers as faculty before moving into administrative jobs. However, tenure as faculty has tended to be relatively short, with only about 17% reporting more than 10 years faculty experience. The first administrative position for most presidents was at the level of chair or dean (about 70%). Some presidents (about 17%) began their administrative career below that level, for example as coordinators or directors of specific programs. A few (less than 3%) entered administration at the higher level of vice president or provost. The last administrative position before presidency—the springboard to the highest position in the academic hierarchy—has been, as might be expected, vice president

Table 4.2 *Educational profile for African American presidents of HBCUs*

Characteristics	Frequency	Percentage
Bachelors Degree		
BA	41	56.94
BS	31	43.06
Total	72	100.00
Undergraduate Institution		
HBCU	47	65.28
Ivy League	1	1.39
Non-HBCU	23	31.94
Not available	1	1.39
Total	72	100.00
Masters Degree		
MA	34	47.22
MS	21	29.17
Other	6	8.33
Not available	11	15.28
Total	72	100.00
Masters Institution		
HBCU	10	13.89
Ivy League	6	8.33
Other	42	58.33
Not available	14	19.45
Total	72	100.00
Terminal Degree		
PhD	44	61.11
EDD	15	20.84
JD	5	6.94
Other	5	6.94
Not available	3	4.17
Total	72	100.00
Terminal Degree Institution		
HBCU	7	9.72
Ivy League	8	11.11
Other	51	70.84
Not available	6	8.33
Total	72	100.00
Academic Discipline		
Education	29	40.28
Social Sciences	11	15.28
Natural Sciences/Math	11	15.28
Business	4	5.56
Other	9	12.50
Not available	8	11.10
Total	72	100.00

Table 4.3 *Career related characteristics of African American presidents of HBCUs*

Characteristics	Frequency	Percentage
Additional Training		
Yes	37	51.39
Not reported	35	48.61
Total	72	100.00
Faculty Experience		
1-10	39	54.17
Greater than 10	12	16.67
None reported	21	29.16
Total	72	100.00
HBCU Experience		
None	8	11.11
1-10	32	44.44
11-20	19	26.39
Greater than 20	5	6.94
Not Reported	8	11.12
Total	72	100.00
Non-HBCU Experience		
None	26	36.11
Less than 10 years	24	33.33
10 or More Years	22	30.56
Total	72	100.00
Entry Position		
Faculty	41	56.94
Administrative	16	22.22
Other	15	20.84
Total	72	100.00
First Administrative Position		
Below Chair	12	16.67
Chair/Director	27	37.50
Dean	23	31.94
Vice Pres./Provost	2	2.78
Non Academic	4	5.56
Not Available	4	5.55
Total	72	100.00
Last Position before Presidency		
Below Chair	1	1.39
Chair/Director	3	4.17
Dean	22	30.56
Vice Pres./Provost	23	31.94
Non Academic	6	8.33
President	13	18.06
Not Available	4	5.55
Total	72	100.00

Continued from previous page

Leadership Positions in Civic/Professional Orgs.		
None reported	8	11.11
1-4	44	61.11
5-8	19	26.39
9 or more	1	1.39
Total	72	100.00

or provost in about 32% of the cases, although an almost equal percentage of presidents (about 31%) were appointed from their position as dean. A few presidents (about 6%) held positions below dean at the time of their appointments. Eighteen percent moved laterally from presidential positions at other institutions.

In general, African American presidents of HBCUs tended to have substantial work experience, as faculty or administrators, in both HBCU and non-HBCU institutions before becoming an HBCU president. However, the overall pattern for HBCU presidents shows greater experience at HBCUs than at non-HBCUs. Relatively few (11%) reported no prior work experience at HBCUs, while more than a third reported no work experience at non-HBCUs.

Table 4.3 summarizes data about the organizational involvement of presidents in professional and civic organizations. As might be expected of presidents as community leaders, African American presidents of HBCUs are not only members of various organizations, but have held leadership positions in many of them. For example, almost 90% of these presidents had served in key positions in various professional and civic organizations. More than 25% held key positions in five or more organizations. The majority are also members of at least one African American organization.

Research Question 2

Is there a relationship between the educational disciplines of African American presidents of historically black colleges and universities and their upward professional mobility?

Research Question 2 required data needed for examining the relationship between the academic discipline (education, social sciences, natural sciences, and business) of African American Presidents and their rate of upward mobility (high, medium, and low) in the career hierarchy. The cross tabulation results presented in Table 4.4 show some variation in the mobility rate based on the academic discipline. This reveals that a greater percentage of presidents who specialized in education show high and medium mobility compared to those who specialized in other disciplines.

The use of the chi-square test, however, provided no statistical significance for the relationship, $\chi^2(df = 15, N = 72) = 6.426, p = .972$. The null hypothesis states that there will be no statistically significant relationship between the educational disciplines of African American presidents of historically black colleges and universities and their upward professional mobility. This hypothesis was not rejected. Therefore, the rate of mobility of these presidents does not depend upon the academic discipline.

Table 4.4 *Relationship between academic discipline and mobility*

	Education		Social Science		Natural Science		Business		Other		Not Available	
	f	%	f	%	f	%	f	%	f	%	f	%
Mobility												
High	9	31.1	4	36.4	4	36.4	2	50.0	2	22.2	4	50.0
Medium	12	41.4	4	14.3	5	45.5	2	50.0	3	33.3	2	25.0
Low	7	24.1	2	18.2	2	18.2	0	0	3	33.3	2	25.0
NA	1	3.4	1	9.1	0	0	0	0	1	11.1	0	0

Research Question 3

Is there a gender-based difference among presidents of historically black colleges and universities in terms of (a) training in certain academic disciplines and (b) the rate of upward mobility?

Research Question 3 dealt with data necessary to investigate the relationship between (a) gender of presidents and their academic discipline, and (b) the gender of presidents and their upward career mobility. The result based on the cross tabulation analysis of the academic discipline between African American male presidents and female presidents of HBCUs indicates that both groups have mostly specialized in Education. However, the percentage of the female presidents who specialized in Education (43.8%) is slightly higher than the percentage of the male presidents with the same academic discipline (39.3%). The results are presented in table 4.5.

Pearson Chi-square test results reveal no statistical significance in differences, $\chi^2(df = 5, N = 72) = 4.3999, p = .493$. The null hypothesis that there will be no statistically significant gender-based difference among presidents of the historically black colleges and universities in terms of training in certain academic disciplines failed to be rejected. Thus, gender of presidents is independent of the academic discipline they choose in their career.

The use of cross tabulation analysis of mobility rates between African American male and female presidents reveals that a greater percentage of male presidents have achieved a high rate of mobility than women presidents (41% and 12.5%). The results are presented in Table 4.6. Chi-square test for the statistical significance between mobility rates of men and women presidents indicates that the relationship is statistically significant, $\chi^2(df = 3, N = 72) = 10.936, p = .012$. The null hypothesis that there will be no statistically significant gender-based difference in upward professional mobility of African American presidents of historically black colleges and universities was rejected. The degree of mobility varies according to gender of presidents.

Table 4.5 *Summary of gender and academic discipline*

	Male		Female	
Discipline	f	%	f	%
Education	22	39.3	7	43.8
Soc. Science	8	14.3	3	18.8
Nat. Science	9	16.0	2	12.5
Business	2	3.6	2	12.5
Other	7	12.4	2	12.4
Not Available	8	14.3	0	0

Table 4.6 *Relationship between gender and mobility*

	Male		Female	
Mobility rate	f	%	f	%
High	23	41.1	2	12.5
Medium	22	39.3	6	37.5
Low	8	14.3	8	50.0
NA	3	5.4	0	0

Research Question 4

Do African American presidents of historically black colleges and universities with additional study/training beyond their degree of discipline ascend the administrative career ladder faster?

This research question involved data necessary for examining the relationship between mobility rates of African American presidents and additional training beyond their degree of discipline. A cross tabulation analysis was performed to investigate the relationship. Table 4.7 contains the result. It should be noted that, of the 72 individuals in the sample, 51% reported additional training. About 73% of those who reported additional training showed high or medium mobility rates. Based on the result of the cross tabulation analysis and the use of the chi square to test the statistical significance of the result, additional training and the mobility rate of presidents are significantly related. The relationship between them is statistically significant, $\chi^2(df = 3, N = 72) = 8.946, p = .030$. The null hypothesis that there will be no statistically significant difference in the rate of ascension of African American presidents of historically black colleges and universities with additional study/training beyond their degree of discipline and those without was rejected. Additional training seems to have an impact on the administrative career mobility of these presidents.

Table 4.7 *Relationship between additional training and mobility*

	Yes		Not Reported	
Mobility rate	f	%	f	%
High	18	48.7	7	20.0
Medium	9	24.3	19	54.3
Low	9	24.3	7	20.0
NA	1	2.7	2	5.7

Research Question 5

Is there a difference in the upward mobility of African American presidents of historically black colleges and universities in regard to (a) marital status, (b) age, and (c) state of origin?

Research Question 5 dealt with data necessary for evaluating the impact of certain selected demographic characteristics of presidents, such as marital status, age, and region of origin on their upward mobility. Cross tabulation analysis was used to evaluate each relationship individually. The results are presented in tables 4.8 through 4.10.

The result of the cross tabulation analysis to examine the relationship between marital status and upward mobility is presented in table 4.8. A greater percentage of presidents who are married seem to have achieved high and medium mobility in their career compared to those who are single and divorced. About 36% and 40%, respectively, of presidents in the married category show high and medium mobility.

The Pearson chi-square test result reveals a statistical significance in the relationship between president's marital status and mobility rates, $\chi^2(df = 6, N = 72) = 17.555, p = .007$. The null hypothesis that states that there will be no statistically significant difference in the upward mobility of African American presidents of historically black colleges and universities with regard to marital status was rejected. Thus, data supports that marriage is a determining factor in the mobility rates of African American presidents of HBCUs.

It may be noted here that cross tabulation analysis reveals that a higher percentage of male presidents are married compared to female presidents. However, based on the chi-square test, the relationship between the gender of presidents and marital status was not statistically significant.

Table 4.9 contains the result of the cross tabulation analysis that was performed to examine the relationship between the age of presidency and rates of upward mobility. About 86% of presidents who are within the age range of 40-49 show high and medium rate of upward mobility. The chi square test revealed that the relationship between age of presidency and upward mobility is statistically significant, $\chi^2(df = 12, N = 72) = 30.047, p = .003$. The null hypothesis that there will be no statistically significant difference in the upward mobility of African American presidents of historically black colleges and universities with regard to age at presidency was rejected. Although, according to frequency distribution, most African Americans assumed presidency between 40 and 69, the mobility rate is higher between ages 40 and 49 compared to other age groups.

Table 4.8 *Relationship between marital status and mobility*

Mobility rate	Married		Divorced		Not reported	
	f	%	f	%	f	%
High	20	36.4	1	20	4	33.3
Medium	22	40.0	1	20	5	41.7
Low	12	21.08	1	20	3	25.0
NA	1	1.8	2	40	0	0

The use of cross tabulation analysis and chi-square test revealed no statistically significant relationship between current age of African American presidents and upward mobility, $\chi^2(df = 12, N = 72) = 15.158, p = .233$. The null hypothesis that there will be no statistically significant difference in upward mobility of African American presidents of historically black colleges and universities with regard to current age failed to be rejected. Thus, president's current age is not a predictor of the rate of upward mobility.

Table 4.9 *Relationship between age at presidency and mobility*

Mobility rate	30-39		40-49		50-59		60-69		70-79	
	f	%	f	%	f	%	f	%	f	%
High	5	62.5	11	37.9	8	26.7	0	0	1	50.0
Med.	1	12.5	14	48.3	12	40.0	1	33.3	0	0
Low	1	12.5	4	13.8	10	33.3	1	33.3	0	0
NA	1	12.5	0	0	0	0	1	33.3	1	50.0

The result of cross tabulation to examine the relationship between region of origin and upward mobility is presented in table 4.10. A greater percentage of African American presidents of HBCUs who were born in the south have achieved high and medium mobility compared to those in other regions. However, the chi-square test revealed no statistically significant relationship between state of origin and mobility rates, $\chi^2(df = 15, N = 72) = 13.881, p = .535$. The null hypothesis that there will be no statistically significant difference in the upward mobility of African American presidents of historically black colleges and universities with regard to state of origin failed to be rejected. The region of origin does not appear to have an impact on rate of mobility.

Research Question 6

Is there a relationship between the position of entry in the professional career of African American presidents of HBCUs and their upward mobility?

Table 4.10 *Relationship between region of origin and mobility*

Mobility rate	West		South		East		Midwest		North		Not available	
	f	%	f	%	f	%	f	%	f	%	f	%
High	3	50.0	9	28.1	1	50.0	4	30.8	5	38.5	3	50.0
Medium	3	50.0	12	37.5	1	50.0	4	30.8	5	38.5	3	50.0
Low	0	0	11	34.4	0	0	3	23.0	2	15.4	0	0
NA	0	0	0	0	0	0	2	15.4	1	7.6	0	0

This research question dealt with data needed to examine the relationship between the entry position of African American presidents of HBCUs and their upward mobility. The cross tabulation analysis of the mobility rates of these presidents reveals that a greater percent of presidents who have entered their career as faculty members show high and medium level of mobility compared to those who started their career as either administrators or in other positions. The results are presented in table 4.11. Based on the chi-square test, the relationship between the position of entry and upward mobility of these presidents is statistically significant, χ^2 ($df = 6$, $N = 72$) = 16.973, $p = .009$. The null hypothesis that there will be no statistically significant relationship between the position of entry in the professional career of African American presidents of historically black colleges and universities and their upward mobility was rejected. Therefore, presidents' position of entry in their professional career is a determining factor in upward mobility.

Table 4.11 *Summary of presidents' position of entry into career and mobility*

Mobility rate	Faculty		Administration		Other	
	f	%	f	%	f	%
High	16	38.1	3	18.7	6	42.9
Medium	16	38.1	8	50.0	4	28.6
Low	10	23.8	5	31.3	1	7.1
NA	0	0	0	0	3	21.4

Research Question 7

What differentiates African American presidents of historically black colleges and universities from African American presidents of traditionally white institutions in terms of their upward professional mobility?

Analysis of Data

This research question requires data, as appropriate, to examine the difference between African American presidents of HBCUs and African American presidents of traditionally white institutions in terms of rates and patterns of their upward mobility in the administrative career hierarchy. The differences are identified and examined in areas of commonalities along demographic, educational, and career related dimensions on the basis of noticeable trends in the data. In addition, differences are examined in terms of significant relationship between selected characteristics of presidents and their upward mobility.

Figures 4.1 through 4.4 present a comparative view of data on certain demographic characteristics, such as age, gender, and region of origin pertaining to African American presidents of traditionally white institutions and those of HBCUs. Figure 4.1 shows data on the age of African American presidents of traditionally white institutions at the time the study was conducted. It indicates that the highest percentage (50%) of these presidents is within the age group of 60-69, compared to presidents of HBCUs who are concentrated within the age range 50-59. The age at which these presidents achieved their presidency is shown in figure 4.2. About 50 percent of African American presidents of TWIs assumed presidency at the age of 40-49, compared with only 40 percent of those at HBCUs within the same age group.

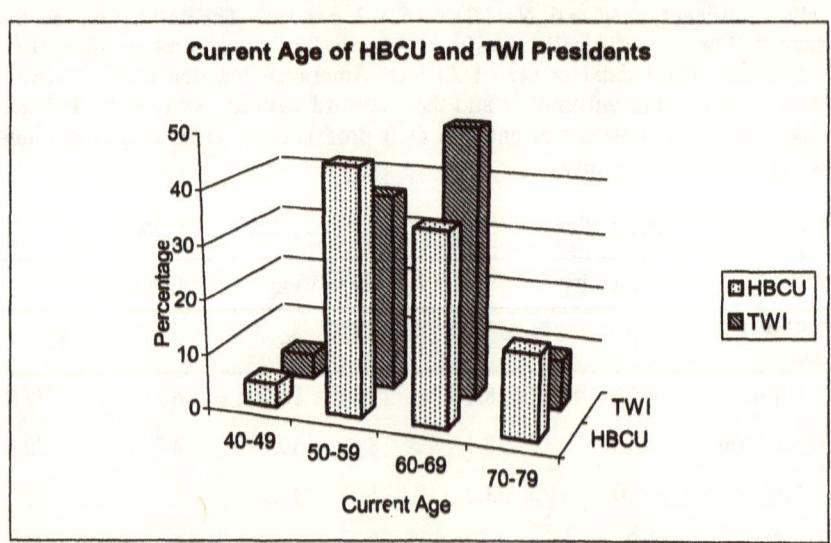

Figure 4.1 Current age of African American HBCU and TWI presidents

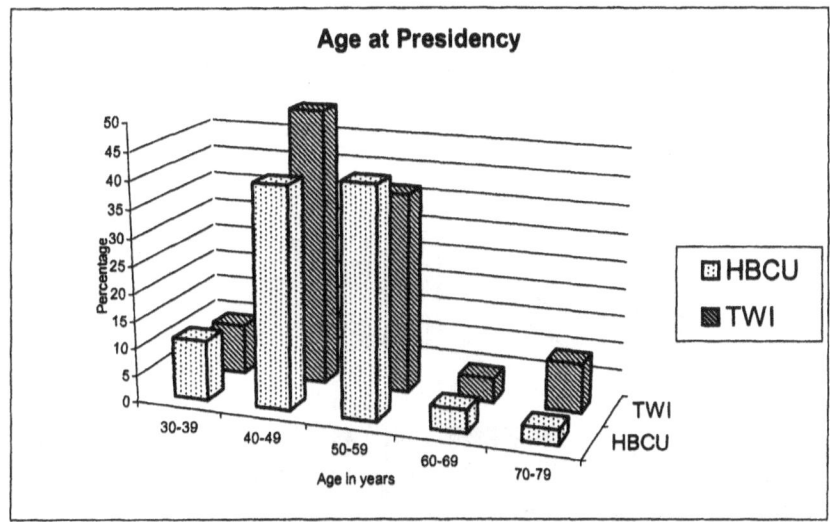

Figure 4.2 Age at presidency of African American HBCU and TWI presidents

Almost 45% of African American presidents of HBCUs were born in the South, and about 36% report the region of birth as Midwest and North. The remainder of those for whom this information is available were born in the East or West. In contrast, African American TWI presidents are almost evenly spread across the United States. This information is shown in figure 4.3.

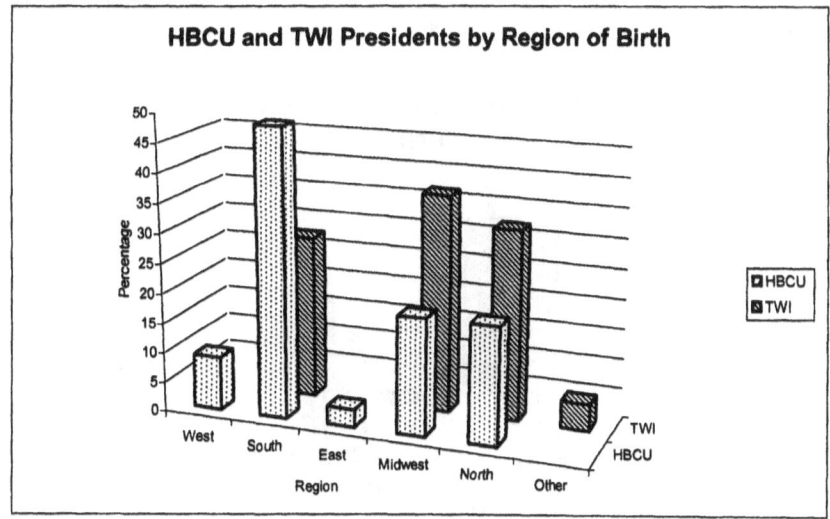

Figure 4.3 Region of birth for African American HBCU and TWI presidents

Based on figure 4.4, the ratio of male to female presidents of HBCUs is higher (77.8%/22.2%) than that of presidents of TWIs (63.6%/36.4%). The percentage of female presidents in TWIs is about 36% compared to 22% at HBCUs.

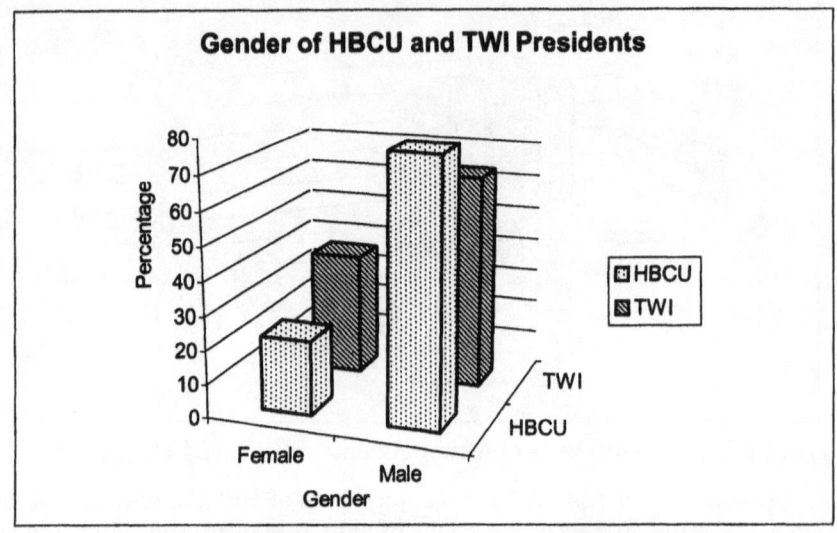

Figure 4.4 Gender of African American HBCU and TWI presidents

Data on educational background reveals few differences between presidents of HBCUs and presidents of TWIs (figures 4.5 and 4.6). For example, about 59 % of African American presidents of TWIs received their undergraduate degree from HBCUs compared with about 65% of presidents of HBCUs.

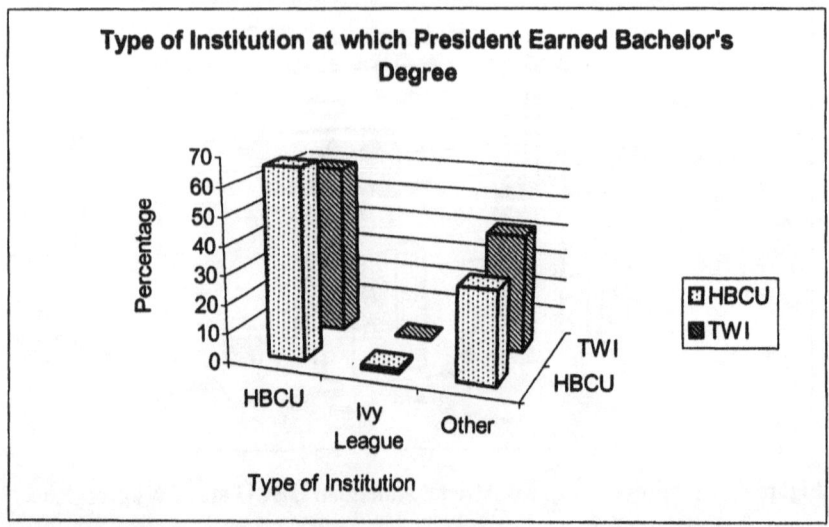

Figure 4.5 Institutions at which presidents earned their bachelor's degree

The difference in institutional types is even more pronounced in masters and doctoral levels. Only 4.5% of presidents of TWIs earned masters degrees from HBCUs compared with 14% of presidents of HBCUs receiving the degree from HBCUs. None of the African American presidents of TWIs had received terminal degree at HBCUs, while about 10% of presidents of HBCUs were granted the degree from HBCUs.

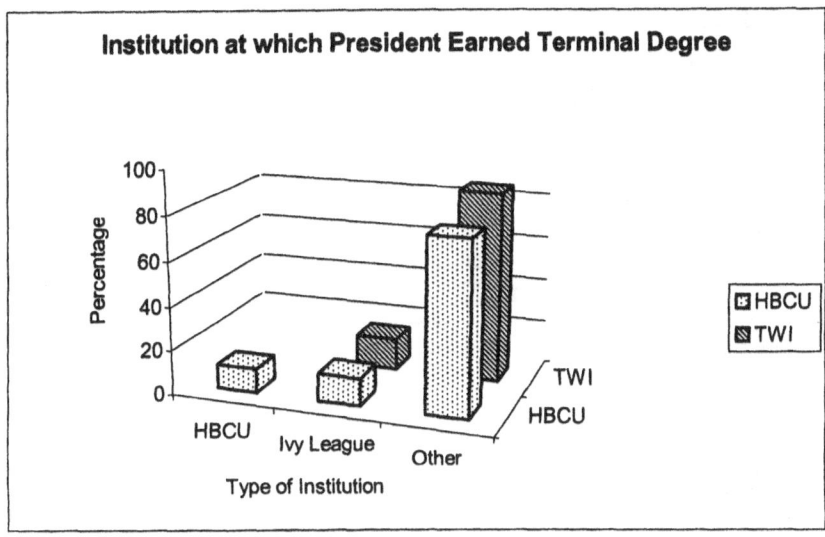

Figure 4.6 Institutions at which presidents earned their terminal degree

The percentage of African American presidents of TWIs holding a Ph.D is about 91%. That is considerably higher than the percentage of presidents of of HBCUs who hold PhDs. Data further indicate that the percentages of African American presidents of HBCUs and TWIs with an Ed.D. are 21% and 5%, respectively. Figure 4.7 represents this difference graphically

Based on data reflected in frequency distribution, African American presidents of TWIs and HBCUs show some career related differences as well. A higher percentage of presidents of HBCUs (about 51%) reported receiving additional training and studies during their administrative career compared to only about 14% of those at TWIs. Data further suggest that the number of presidents of TWIs is higher than the number of presidents of HBCUs in terms of faculty experiences, but considerably lower in terms of professional experiences at HBCUs. For example, about 77% of African American presidents of TWIs did not have any professional experience at HBCUs prior to their presidency. For presidents of HBCUs, only 11% did not have any experience at HBCUs. Figure 4.8 shows the professional experience of African American Presidents at HBCUs. Figure 4.9 shows the professional experience at non-HBCUs.

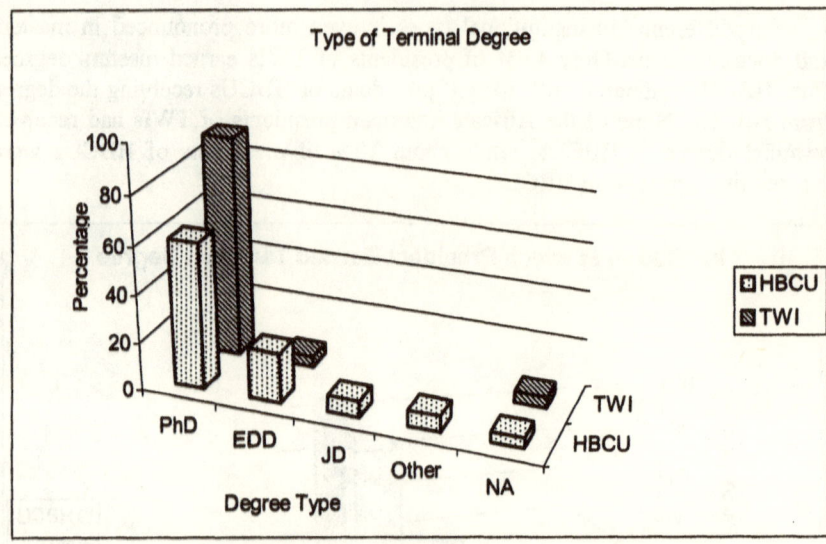

Figure 4.7 Type of terminal degree earned by African American presidents

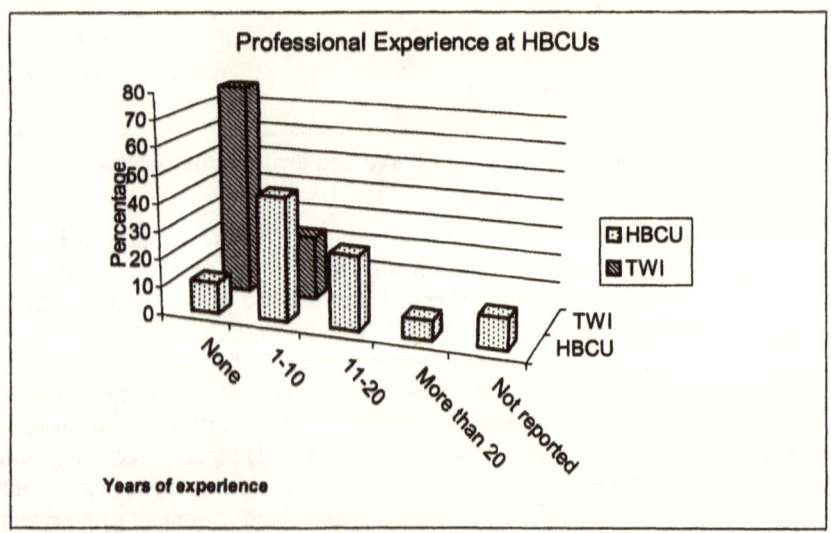

Figure 4.8 Professional experience at HBCUs

Along the same line, it may be noted that about 50% of presidents of TWIs gained 10 or more years of professional experience at non HBCUs. Only about 27% of these presidents reported having no experience at non- HBCUs. Figure 4.9 shows this data graphically.

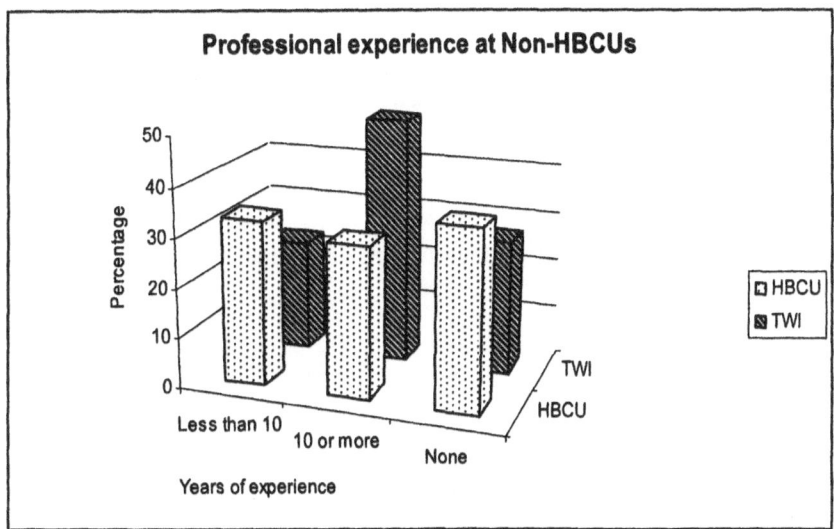

Figure 4.9 Professional experience at non-HBCUs

Comparative data on position of entry for African American presidents of TWIs and HBCUs are shown in figure 4.10. About 50% of African American presidents of TWIs entered their careers as faculty compared with 32% who entered as administrators. The percentages of faculty and administrative positions as entry positions for presidents of HBCUs were about 58% and 22%, respectively.

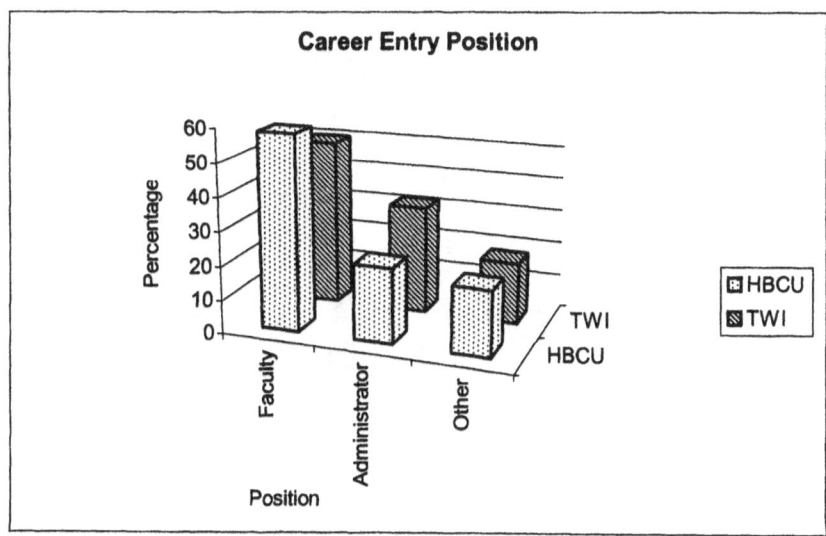

Figure 4.10. Entry position for African American presidents.

Figure 4.11 shows the first administrative position for African American presidents. None of the presidents of TWIs started their first administrative job below the position of chair. Additionally, the number of presidents of TWIs with a first administrative job as chair, director, or dean is about 91%, that is much higher than 69% of presidents of HBCUs who had assumed similar administrative positions as their first.

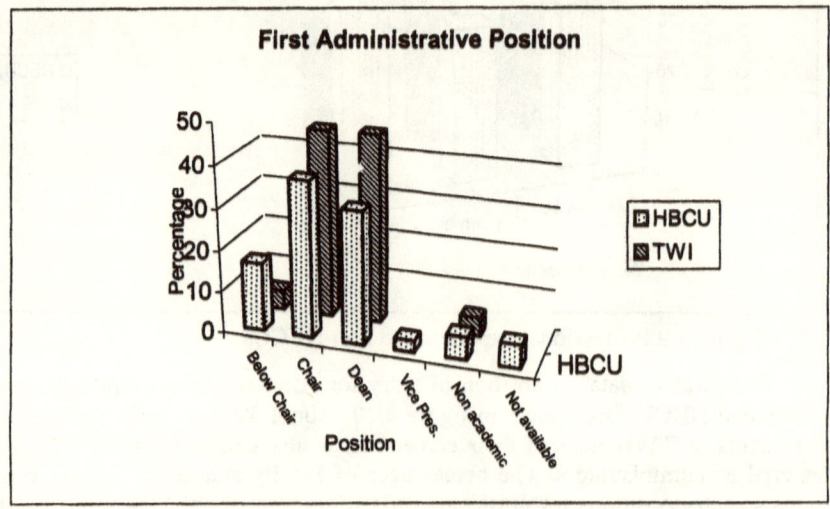

Figure 4.11. First administrative position for African American presidents

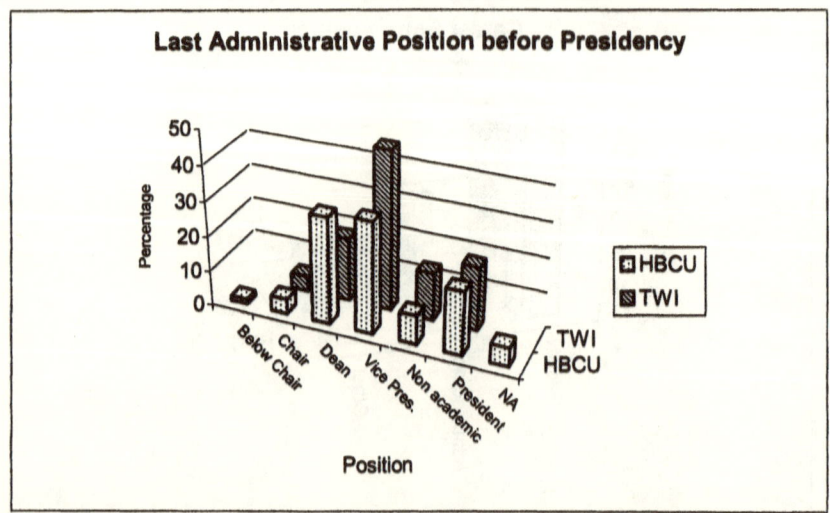

Figure 4.12. Last position before presidency for African American presidents

Figure 4.12 shows the last position held before becoming president. Most African American presidents (about 46%) of TWIs were provosts or vice presidents prior to their presidency compared to 32% of presidents of HBCUs. However, the percentages of African American presidents of both TWIs and HBCUs with last administrative positions as dean, vice president, or provost before presidency are about the same.

Data on positions held in professional and community organizations indicate that African American presidents of both TWIs and HBCUs hold several key positions in various organizations. However, a higher number (about 49%) of African American presidents of TWIs, on average, hold about 5 to 8 key positions compared to about 27% of presidents of HBCUs in that category. These data are presented graphically in figure 4.13.

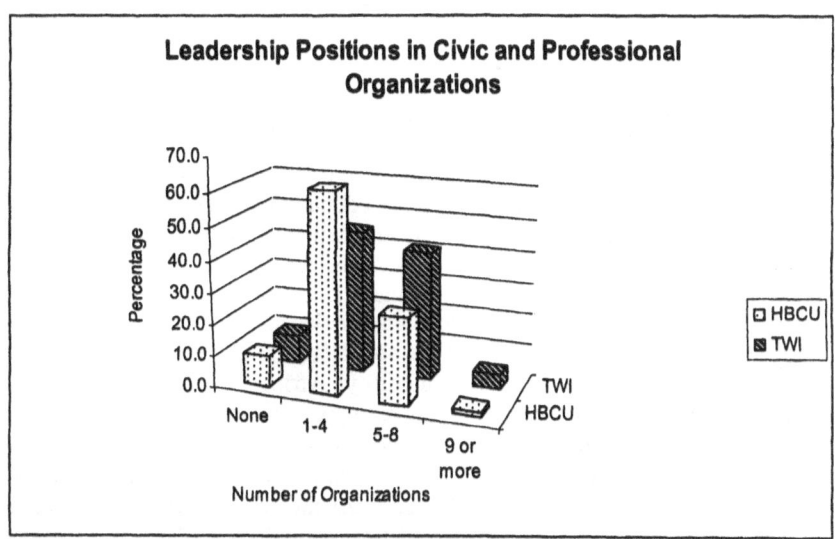

Figure 4.13. Leadership positions in civic and professional organizations

The relationships that were found to be statistically significant for African American presidents of HBCUs but not for African American presidents of TWIs, were between (a) age at presidency and upward mobility, (b) additional training and rate of mobility, and (c) position of entry into professional career and rate of mobility.

The use of cross tabulation analysis of mobility rates between African American presidents of HBCUs and TWIs indicates that a greater percentage of TWI presidents have achieved higher rates of mobility than presidents of HBCUs. The results are presented in Table 4.12. Based on the chi square test, the relationship between the institutional types and upward mobility of these presidents is not statistically significant, $\chi^2(df = 3, N = 94) = 6.564, p = .087$. The null hypothesis that there will be no statistically significant relationship between African American presidents of HBCUs and TWIs in terms of upward professional mobility failed to be rejected. The rate of mobility of presidents does not differ based on the types of institution they lead.

Table 4.12 *Relationship between institutional types and upward mobility*

Mobility rate	HBCU		TWI	
	f	%	f	%
High	25	34.7	14	63.6
Medium	28	38.9	4	18.2
Low	16	22.2	4	18.2
Not available	3	4.2	0	0

Ancillary Analyses

Cross tabulation analyses were performed on data needed to examine the relationship between selected demographic, educational, and career related variables and the mobility of African American presidents of TWIs and compare the results with those analyzed for African American presidents of HBCUs. Chi square tests were also used to identify the relationships with statistical significance. The overall results showed few similarities and few differences between African American presidents of TWIs and HBCUs, in terms of relationships between certain characteristics and mobility. African American presidents of both TWIs and HBCUs showed similar patterns in terms of the relationship between (a) gender and upward mobility, and (b) marital status and upward mobility. For both groups, the relationships were statistically significant. In addition, it should be noted that the relationship between the gender and marital status for presidents of TWIs was found to be statistically significant. Tables 4.13 through 4.15 show the results of cross tabulation analyses that were performed to examine the relationships between (a) gender and upward mobility, (b) marital status and mobility, and (c) gender and marital status for African American presidents of TWIs.

Table 4.13 *Relationship between gender and mobility for TWI presidents*

Mobility rate	Male		Female	
	f	%	f	%
High	10	71.4	4	50.0
Medium	0	0	4	50.0
Low	4	28.6	0	0

Table 4.14 *Relationship between marital status and mobility for TWI presidents*

	Married		Single		Widowed		Not reported	
Mobility rate	f	%	f	%	f	%	f	%
High	9	64.3	0	0	0	0	5	100
Med.	1	7.1	2	100	1	100	0	0
Low	4	28.6	0	0	0	0	0	0

Table 4.15 *Relationship between gender and marital status of African American presidents of TWIs*

	Male		Female	
Mobility rate	f	%	f	%
Married	12	85.7	2	25.0
Single	0	0	2	25.0
Widowed	0	0	1	12.5
Not reported	2	14.3	3	37.5

Chi-square tests revealed statistically significant relationships between gender and upward mobility, $\chi^2(df = 2, N = 22) = 9.653, p = .008$; between marital status and upward mobility, $\chi^2(df = 6, N = 22) = 18.128, p = .006$; and between gender and marital status, $\chi^2(df = 3, N = 22) = 9.406, p = .024$. Therefore, the null hypotheses that gender is independent on either marital status or mobility and marital status is independent on mobility were rejected.

Chapter 5

Summary, Conclusions, Implications, and Recommendations

This investigation has focused on the upward mobility of African American university presidents in their administrative careers, with particular emphasis on presidents of historically black colleges and universities (HBCUs). This final chapter includes a summary of the research study, followed by a discussion of the findings and interpretations pertaining to research questions based on data analysis. Findings associated with career mobility and labor market components are presented, as well as ancillary findings derived from the study. Chapter 5 also outlines the potential implications of such findings on policy formulation and practice in the general area of educational administration. Finally, the chapter identifies certain limitations of this study and makes recommendations for future research.

Summary

In view of the myriad changes and challenges in institutions of higher education in general and historically black colleges and universities in particular, the roles and responsibilities of contemporary presidents of these institutions are not only changing, but are considered more important and serious than ever before (Duderstadt 2000a). In fact, presidents have been subjected to a fair amount of scrutiny in recent years (Birnbaum 1999). Therefore, a great deal of emphasis is placed on a careful analysis and application of certain criteria such as mobility patterns for examining the success and effectiveness of these presidents as academic leaders (Hahn 1995).

This study investigated the trend, pattern, and rate of upward mobility of African American presidents of colleges and universities during their rise to presidency. Given the vital role of African American HBCU presidents in higher education and the limited literature available, this study focused on an analysis of their upward mobility. In sum, the study attempted to (a) identify and examine specific trends and patterns of mobility by determining common traits, characteristics, and behaviors of African American presidents; (b) examine the rate of upward mobility among African American presidents on the basis of certain demographic, educational and career related characteristics; and (c) compare African American presidents of HBCUs and TWIs (traditionally white institutions) in terms of significant trends in their biographical characteristics and significant relationships between their biographical characteristics and upward mobility.

A review of literature, deemed appropriate for this study, was conducted for career-related subjects such as career mobility, career achievement, glass ceilings, career paths, discrimination, and labor market theories. Literature was collected and presented in specific areas, including presidents in higher education, women and minority presidents in higher education, the role of historically black colleges and universities and their presidents, and the relevant theoretical framework applicable to these areas.

The study utilized unobtrusive biographical data on African American presidents of HBCUs and data collected from available public archival sources. The primary data sources for demographic, educational, career, and organizational data included reports of *National Association for Equal Opportunity* (NAFEO profile 2002), annual directories such as *Who's Who among African Americans* (Bennett et. al. 2001; Henderson and York 2002) and *Who's Who in America* (2002). In addition, journals, magazines, newsletter and Internet websites served as supplementary data sources. Approximately 72 HBCUs and 22 TWIs constituted the sample size for the study populations.

This study included both quantitative and qualitative approaches to accomplish its objectives. Data were analyzed by using descriptive statistics, including frequencies and percentages, for each predictor variable to identify certain trends and patterns relative to presidential career mobility. Cross tabulations and chi-square tests assisted in determining significant relationships between selected demographic, educational, and career related variables and the rate of upward mobility of African American presidents of HBCUs and TWIs.

Research Findings

The research findings and interpretations must be viewed and evaluated within the parameters set by the study's limitations and delimitations (e.g., current presidents of HBCUs and TWIs with available biographical information).

Research Question 1

Research Question 1 deals with commonalities in demographic, educational, and career related profiles of HBCU African American presidents. The findings suggest that there are common characteristics among presidents along each of these dimensions.

Most African American presidents of HBCUs are in their 50s. The majority of them assumed the presidency in their 40s and 50s. A study on four-year colleges, conducted by Wessel and Keim (1994), revealed a mean age of 47 for presidential inaugurations. However, the growth in the number of presidents that assumed the presidency in their 50s may be the result of a new wave of African American presidents at HBCUs with diverse administrative experiences and career paths who have been appointed within the last 5 years (New black college presidents 1999).

Summary, Conclusions, Implications, and Recommendations 61

The profound gender gap among African American presidents of HBCUs mirrors the pattern found among college and university presidents in higher education as a whole. One particular study indicated that women, in general, continue to be perceived as effective instructors but not effective administrators in society (Ortiz and Marshall 1988). The study further revealed that very few women held senior positions in the administrative hierarchy. According to Coleman (1998), African American women administrators perceive negative attitudes of male administrators toward women as a barrier in their administrative career success. Although an increasing number of women are becoming presidents in recent years, the rate of increase continues to be small (Corrigan 2002).

The majority of presidents were born in the South. The Midwest and the North hold the second rank in terms of presidents' birth regions. The fewest number of these presidents were born in the East and West.

A significant number of presidents of HBCUs are married. This trend may be explained as a part of the larger need for a support system by these top level administrators. In performing complex and demanding leadership roles, presidents of colleges and universities require a strong support system around them (Dill 1984). Dill explains that the longer hours per week, frequent out of town trips, and considerable amount of time spent with other administrators clearly justify the need for a powerful support system. Family and community are important parts of this support system. Interestingly, however, approximately 18% fewer female presidents are married compared to their male counterparts.

Findings related to the educational attainment of African American presidents of HBCUs show certain commonalities, particularly in terms of the types of institutions attended in the undergraduate and graduate levels. The majority of these presidents received their undergraduate degrees from HBCUs. This may be a residual outcome of the pre-Civil Rights era when African Americans could only attend HBCUs for higher education (Williams 1988). HBCUs were instrumental in liberating and empowering African American aspirations for the American dream (Allen and Jewell 2002). Yet most of these presidents earned their masters and doctoral degrees from universities other than HBCUs and ivy league schools. This trend is not surprising because there were few HBCUs offering masters and doctoral programs, leaving almost no option for aspiring administrators in the selection process. Even today there are but a handful of HBCUs offering masters degrees and even fewer that grant doctoral degrees (Williams 1988). A greater number of presidents seem to have preferred majoring in the arts since the majority earned bachelors of arts and masters of arts degrees.

Almost all presidents earned terminal degrees before ascending to the presidency. In addition, a significant number of these presidents hold a Ph.D. as their terminal degree with education as their specialized field of study. Traditionally, specialization in education has been associated with teaching. While earlier studies on minority presidents had identified and suggested doctoral degrees for minority administrators in order to attain senior level positions (Esquibel 1997), the terminal degree seems to be an absolute necessity in these times for reaching the pinnacle of an administrative career (Altbach, Lomotey, and Kyle 1999). A survey of 106 doctoral degree recipients indicated the importance of the terminal degree for attaining administrative jobs as well as developing self confidence (King and Chepyator 1996).

There are commonalities in career related characteristics that signify certain trends and patterns for African American presidents of HBCUs. These pertain to their training, professional experiences, and participation in various professional, community, and civic organizations.

Over half of the presidents in the study received additional training in the form of either management experience or further studies prior to becoming president. Findings of certain studies suggest that a president's formal education is not adequate to deal with the complexities associated with effective academic leadership (McDade 1988).

The most common entry position in the careers of African American presidents of HBCUs is the faculty. A faculty position seems to be the passport to an administrative job (Townsend 1996). A high percentage of presidents enter their first administrative job as either a chair or director; whereas, the last position prior to presidency held by most is that of vice president/provost or dean. An increasing number of presidents moved laterally from a presidential position at other colleges and universities (Corrigan 2002). This is consistent with Vaughan (1990) who claims that there is a clear presidential pipeline or pathway via the senior academic officer's position in higher education.

A significant number of African American presidents of HBCUs have served as faculty members in various colleges and universities prior to moving into administrative positions. There is strong evidence of faculty experience being a contributing factor to good administration (Rolle, Davis, and Banning 2000). It is important to know that many presidents continued to teach throughout their administrative careers. Although these presidents have gained years of professional experience in both HBCUs and non-HBCUs, their collective experience at HBCUs is significantly greater than that at non-HBCUs. In fact, only a few African American HBCU presidents reported no professional experience at HBCUs. This finding is supported by the fact that presidents of colleges and universities are expected to learn the specific institutional culture in order to become effective players (Rolle, Davies, and Banning 2000). In addition, presidents receive a sense of belonging, responsibility, and a support system at HBCUs (Frierson 1993).

African American presidents of HBCUs generally hold membership in many various professional, civic, and community organizations. In addition, most of them are members of at least one African American organization. Undoubtedly, presidents need community support, an opportunity for mentoring, and networking for successful leadership (Jones 2001).

Research Question 2

This question deals with the relationship between educational disciplines of African American HBCU presidents and their corresponding upward mobility. The hypothesis is that there is no statistically significant relationship between these two variables. However, based on the findings of this research, the hypothesis failed to be rejected. Although a high percentage of presidents who specialized in education showed some level of mobility, the relationship between academic discipline and upward mobility was not found to be statistically significant. The result may be attributable to the idea that education as a discipline is not considered adequate to prepare academic leaders to deal effectively with the complexities of administration in higher education; it may actually impede career mobility (Brown, Martinez, and Daniel 2002). Based on findings of a survey of college instructional leaders conducted by these authors, a high percentage of leaders, particularly in community college, view the discipline of education to provide less preparation for an administrative role than other disciplines. However, education continues to receive a higher rating than several recently established specialized fields (Townsend 1996).

Research Question 3

Research Question 3 deals with the relationship between (a) gender and academic discipline, and (b) gender and upward mobility of African American HBCU presidents.

The hypothesis that there is no statistically significant relationship between gender and the academic discipline of African American presidents failed to be rejected. Although the number of women in the discipline of education was slightly higher than that of men, research findings indicate that the difference was not statistically significant.

The hypothesis that there is no statistically significant difference between gender and upward mobility of these presidents was rejected. Findings of studies pertaining to the glass ceiling phenomenon and African American administrators clearly indicate that men attain higher mobility in their careers than women (Coleman 1998; Ramey 1995). Of course, the gender gap among African American presidents in higher education sheds some insight into the existing barriers affecting their administrative career mobility.

In a survey conducted by Ramey (1995), African American women at the dean's level or above at four-year institutions listed sexism as a barrier in HBCUs to their promotions and career advancement. One female participant explained: "It is a constant battle to work through male dominated areas. . . . I need to sometimes work twice as hard. I have difficulty supervising entrenched male groups" (Ramey 1995, 116).

The study identified several other barriers and suggested solutions, such as providing opportunities for networking and training in leadership. The same gender-based pattern with regard to upward mobility was also found among community college presidents.

Research Question 4

This question required the investigation of the relationship between additional study/training (beyond their degree of discipline) received by African American HBCU presidents and the rate of upward mobility.

The hypothesis stated that there is no statistically significant difference between additional study/training beyond the degree of discipline and upward mobility of African American presidents of HBCUs. Based on the findings of this research, the hypothesis was rejected. Additional training or study beyond the formal degree seems to make a difference in the administrative career mobility of these presidents.

This finding supports the conclusions drawn by Cortada (1996), who thought, based on his research, that although academic education is important, management training and studies for improving effective leadership skills is also critical for college and university presidency. A study on minority presidents by Esquibel (1997) identified specific training and management skills as contributing factors toward career mobility. Vaughan and Weisman (1998) found knowledge, skill, and ongoing management training for college presidents to be essential for success in presidential leadership.

Research Question 5

For resolving this question, analysis of the data explored relationships between certain demographic characteristics of African American presidents of HBCUs, such as marital status, age, and state of origin and their upward mobility.

The hypothesis stated that there is no statistically significant difference in upward mobility of African American presidents with regard to marital status. However, based on this research, the hypothesis was rejected. The rate of mobility was higher for those who were married compared to those who were not (Dill 1984).

In his investigation of the effects of marriage partnership on university presidents, Kerr (2001) found that most presidents acknowledged the importance of spousal support on their stability, productivity, success, and professional career. Lopez (1996) identified a similar pattern in his study of career mobility among upper level Hispanic administrators.

The hypothesis that there is no difference in upward mobility of African American presidents based on age when attaining the presidency was also rejected based on this research. A high percentage of African American presidents who were relatively younger achieved a medium or high rate of mobility. The result is consistent with a study by Miklos (1988), which found an association of age of attaining the presidency and the rate of mobility. According to Miklos, formulating career goals and beginning an administrative career at an earlier age contributed to a more rapid rate of upward mobility.

However, the relationship between current age of presidents and upward mobility was not found to be significant. The current age of a president was not a predictor of mobility (Fincher 1997).

Based on the findings of this research, the hypothesis that there is no statistically significant difference in upward mobility of African American presidents with regard to their state of origin was not rejected. The birth state of presidents is not a significant predictor of career mobility. Although most African American presidents of HBCUs were born in the South, this pattern fits the geographical distribution of African Americans in the population of the United States in general.

Research Question 6

This question dealt with the investigation of the relationship between the career entry point of African American HBCU presidents and their upward mobility.

The hypothesis stated that there is no statistically significant relationship between the entry point in the professional career of African American presidents and their upward mobility. Based on the findings of this research, the hypothesis was rejected. The majority of presidents who started their careers as faculty members achieved high and medium rates of mobility in the administrative career hierarchy. This research finding is supported by Kerr and Gade (1986) who suggested, based on their study, that a faculty position was overwhelmingly the entry point for presidents of four-year colleges and universities.

According to Jones (1995), faculty members were usually selected for administrative positions because of their expertise in a particular curriculum, such as business management or finance. He further acknowledges that most institutions' faculty members in general possessed more career options.

Research Question 7

Research Question 7 involved a comparison between African American presidents of HBCUs and TWIs to identify their differences relative to demographic, educational, and career related characteristics as well as the statistically significant relationships in terms of upward mobility. In addition, while comparing the characteristics of presidents of both types of institutions, a few significant relationships were found between certain biographical characteristics and the upward mobility of African American TWI presidents.

A comparison of African American presidents of HBCUs and TWIs revealed certain significant differences in patterns of demographic, educational, and career related characteristics. Most African American presidents of TWIs were 60 to 69 years of age, a higher range than that of HBCU presidents. However, the TWI presidents ascended to the presidency within the same age range as the presidents of HBCUs. Consequently, African American presidents of TWIs appeared to serve longer in their positions compared to HBCU presidents. Of course, the current age of the administrator is simply a measure of experience, not necessarily a predictor of certain patterns of career mobility (Fincher 1997). Unlike African American presidents of HBCUs, African American TWI presidents were born primarily in the Midwest and North. The ratio of male presidents to female presidents was relatively higher at TWIs than at HBCUs. This may be a reflection of the recent increase in the number of African American presidents in higher education (Corrigan 2002).

Differences in educational profiles of African American presidents of HBCUs and TWIs were less pronounced when considering the institutions attended for undergraduate and graduate education, but more pronounced in the type of terminal degree earned. For example, a significant number of African American presidents of TWIs, similarly to HBCU presidents, had received their bachelor's degrees at HBCUs and masters/doctoral degrees at universities other than HBCUs. However, the number of African American TWI presidents that held a Ph.D. was significantly higher than that of African American presidents at HBCUs. This may be the result of specific hiring practices at TWIs, which attracted more leaders with diverse experiences (Wilson 1997).

The phenomenon may be explained by Wilson's study which found that the acquisition of a broad range of human capital credentials and past administrative experiences were more important determinants of movement into upper tier positions for African Americans than for whites. Other explanations may lie in the specific selection criteria used by TWI and HBCU institutions. However, those possible institutional differences lie beyond the scope of this study.

There are profound differences in the trends and patterns of career related profiles between African American presidents of HBCUs and TWIs. For example, a significantly higher number of African American presidents of TWIs had gained years of professional experience at non-HBCUs rather than at HBCUs, compared to presidents of HBCUs. In fact, the number of African American TWI presidents that reported having no experience at HBCUs was found to be considerably higher than the number of HBCU presidents with no experience at non-HBCUs. This may be an indicator of varying degrees of diversity promoted across institutions of higher education (Roach 2000).

Roach explained the continuing effort for hiring presidents with diverse experience at HBCUs. Balancing this search for diversity is the powerful role networking or mentoring may also play in the selection process, enhancing the candidacy of an individual for top-level positions across the institutions in which he or she is best known by virtue of career experience in these institutions. The latter effect is a two-edged sword, in that more years of experience at HBCUs means fewer years of experience and less exposure and networking among non-HBCU institutions. This may actually have had a negative impact on career mobility.

Other career related differences among presidents of both types of institutions were in areas of training beyond the degree of discipline, first administrative position, last administrative position prior to presidency, and positions held in professional/community organizations. Unlike African American presidents of historically black colleges and universities, very few African American presidents of traditionally white institutions had received additional training beyond the degree of discipline.

Some literature pertaining to hiring criteria for upper tier occupations tend to validate this finding. Wilson's study on racial differences in the determinants of job authority is relevant (Wilson 1997). Rolle, Davies, and Banning (2000) also addressed the issue in their article on the experiences of African American administrators at traditionally white institutions.

Although most presidents of TWIs entered their professional career as faculty, as did presidents of HBCUs, a higher number of African American presidents at TWIs began their career in administrative positions compared to those at HBCUs. In fact, the gap between presidents entering as faculty versus administrators was significantly higher for HBCUs compared with TWIs.

An interesting observation from the research was that the most common administrative position held immediately prior to presidency for African American presidents of TWIs was vice president, while the last position common to most presidents of HBCUs was dean. The distinction between African American presidents of HBCUs and TWIs in terms of last position prior to presidency was perhaps based on the difference in entry points of their respective professional careers.

Finally, leadership positions in professional, civic, and community organizations was found to be a key differentiating factor between African American presidents of HBCUs and TWIs. Although African American presidents in both types of institutions held certain key positions in various organizations, more TWI presidents were involved in a greater number of organizations. This finding is reinforced by literature stating that TWIs typically focused on informal network, negotiations, and network of contacts as important aspects of academic administration (Wessel and Keim 1994). African American presidents of these institutions with diverse experiences at similar institutions were expected to have the same focus.

Based on the overall findings of this research, several trends and patterns of differences existed between African American presidents of HBCUs and TWIs in terms of demographic, educational, and career related characteristics associated with career progression.

Differences in upward mobility were sought between African American presidents of HBCUs and TWIs by determining the level of statistical significance. Based on the study, the hypothesis that there are no statistically significant relationships between African American presidents of HBCUs and TWIs in terms of upward professional mobility, failed to be rejected. The mobility rates of these presidents did not depend on the types of institutions they were leading. To some extent, this appears to be inconsistent with the findings of a number of studies that revealed the presence of a glass ceiling in the mobility pattern for

African American administrators at traditionally white universities (Brown 1997, Jones 1995).

This result may be explained by the level of seriousness that educators place on the position of presidency in higher education and on the strict selection criteria for filling that position. In addition, presidents today avail many opportunities to prepare themselves to deal with the complexities facing higher education (Kit 2000). However, it is important to acknowledge the low representation of African American presidents in TWIs. These institutions utilize specific hiring criteria and practices in appointing upper level administrators. According to Rolle, Davies, and Banning (2000), African Americans attained upper tier occupations on the basis of closer scrutiny of formal credentials and related experiences at a similar level at previous institutions. They were also expected to undertake additional challenges. Lindsay (1994) explained that minorities in TWI administration constituted a small number, usually high achievers, and were subject to higher expectations and extensive evaluations.

It may be noted that biographical predictors, such as age of attaining presidency, additional training beyond the primary degree of discipline, and career entry position, which made statistically significant differences in the upward mobility of African American presidents of HBCUs were not determined to be key factors in the impact on the upward mobility of African American presidents of TWIs.

Findings Associated with Career Mobility/Labor Market Components

This study provides some useful insights for understanding the mobility patterns of African American university and college presidents in the context of career mobility and labor market characteristics. Cohen and March (1974) suggested that career mobility follows a normative ladder, defined as a strictly sequential career path from faculty member to president via sequentially higher administrative positions (e.g., chair to dean to vice president/provost). Based on the findings of this research, the career progression of African American college and university presidents, from entry position to first administrative position to last position before presidency, tends to follow that normative pattern, with variation, in that the strict sequence as envisioned by Cohen and March is not always followed.

Wessel and Keim (1994) drew a distinction between academic career paths, which begin with the entry position as faculty, and administrative paths, which begin with the entry position into an administrative job. In this study, the academic career path seemed to be more pronounced for presidents of HBCUs. In contrast, the African American TWI presidents presented a more varied pattern in their career paths.

Certain characteristics of presidents in demographic, educational, and career related areas were found to be predictors of their upward mobility. These findings support the rationale to conduct an individual level of analysis for better insights into the career mobility patterns of administrators in higher education. The relationships between a president's biographical variables and upward mobility fit into the sociological model emphasized by Vardi (1980), which shows that a combination of individual and organizational characteristics captures a clearer understanding of presidential upward mobility.

Research findings on the various positions held by African American presidents prior to their presidency connect to the structural features of internal labor market theory as postulated by Althauser and Kalleberg (1981) and Bills (1987). These features include (a) establishing an entry at a lower level position; (b) advancing through various positions; and (c) progressively developing knowledge and skills—the "human capital" accumulation that qualifies the individual for advancement.

The findings of this study suggest that the career entry level for African American presidents is usually the faculty level. More than half (57%) of the HBCU African American presidents included in this study began their careers as faculty members. Presidents climbed the career ladder progressively through a sequence of administrative positions, such as department chair, dean, and vice president/provost, prior to assuming the presidency. Many of these presidents moved laterally in similar positions to other institutions at some point in their careers. But this pattern of career mobility implied upward movement through a hierarchy of positions in higher education (Vardi 1980). The many years of employment and professional experience gained by African American HBCU and TWI presidents provided the opportunities for increasing knowledge and skills that qualified them for higher positions. Furthermore, gradual progression in the attainment of education reflected an improvement in a president's knowledge base. For example, almost all African American presidents received a Ph.D., on average about eleven years after receiving a masters degree and prior to ascending to the role of president. Many African American presidents obtained additional training beyond the Ph.D. This typical sequence marked a progression in knowledge and skill level via education while continuing forward in their administrative career. The majority of presidents served as either a dean or vice president prior to their role as president. In fact, most presidents held varied administrative positions within higher education. This trend of mobility within the boundary of higher education is consistent with the features of the internal labor market.

Although HBCU presidents demonstrated considerable experience at both HBCU and non-HBCU institutions, their professional experience seemed to be weighted more heavily towards HBCUs. This may be a reflection of a preference of HBCU presidents to serve in institutions similar to ones in which they gained more opportunities and experiences. In sum, the trends and patterns of presidents' mobility seem to meet certain criteria of an internal labor market. However, further in-depth research of the organizational characteristics of HBCUs and an analysis of their presidents' career pattern might be more beneficial in terms of understanding the dynamics of career mobility in the context of labor market. These questions lie beyond the scope of the present study.

Ancillary Findings

In several of the research questions, the population of interest was that of African American presidents of HBCUs, and the questions addressed the relationship between biographical data such as gender and marital status and upward mobility in the sample of that population. Although not part of the research plan, the same relationships were tested for the sample of African American presidents of TWIs. This ancillary analysis identified statistically significant relationships between gender and upward mobility and between marital status and upward mobility in the sample of African American presidents of TWIs. It was interesting to find these relationships that show patterns similar to those of HBCU presidents.

The hypothesis tested was that there is no statistically significant difference in upward mobility of African American presidents of TWIs with regard to gender. Based on this research finding, the hypothesis was rejected. As with the impact on HBCU presidents, gender made a difference in the upward mobility of African American TWI presidents. The result was illustrative of a more general pattern in higher education. Underrepresentation of women in higher education has been attributed to societal and educational values discouraging women in administration and the traditional perception of females as instructors rather than administrators (Ortiz and Marshall 1999). According to these authors, women also lacked credible support in the sponsorship process.

These ideas are supported by the research findings of Ramey (1995). African American women participants in this study viewed sexism, in addition to racism, as a barrier to career advancement. As one participant stated, "Some people have more difficulty dealing with me as a woman than as an African American administrator. Though race was an issue, now I suffer more from a gender issue" (p. 116).

The hypothesis that there is no statistically significant difference in the upward mobility of African American presidents with regard to marital status was also rejected. This pattern of mobility associated with marital status was similar to that of HBCU presidents. A high percentage of presidents of institutions of higher education were married (Corrigan 2002). Unlike with African American HBCU presidents, a statistically significant relationship was found between gender and marital status for TWI presidents. The hypothesis that there is no statistically significant difference in marital status of TWI African American presidents based on gender was rejected. The result is supported by the American Council on Education report (Corrigan 2002). This relationship may be attributed to the increasing amount of pressure that women confront arising from conflicts between their family, career, and work (Ramey 1995).

Implications for Policy and Practice

The following section relates to the implications for education and educational administration based on the research findings. The present study identifies trends and patterns in characteristics that are shared by African American presidents and analyzes their relationship to the individual's upward mobility. Thus this study does have implications for policy and practice in the selection of these individuals.

1. The selection criteria for African Americans who aspire to be presidents of colleges and universities, particularly at HBCUs, should include individuals who have holistic and experiential academic backgrounds, and those who have demonstrated success in positions that require management skills.

2. The candidates for the position of African American HBCU president should have an educational background that reflects management related training and study. In addition, resources for continued professional development and training should be a part of the compensation package for college and university presidents.

3. The present study documents the under representation of African American female administrators in the selection of presidents. This is the so-called "glass ceiling effect." Further studies might look at criteria that directly or indirectly lead to the exclusion of qualified females from the pool of presidential candidates or to their under-selection from the pool.

4. African Americans who aspire to leadership positions in academic institutions should prepare themselves educationally with preferably more holistic academic disciplines. For example, the Ph.D. degree appears to be held more often by presidents than the more specialized Ed.D.

5. African Americans aspiring to ascend the administrative career ladder to the position of president must prepare themselves early in life for this position through faculty and administrative experience at a college or university.

Recommendations for Future Research

The following areas warrant future attention for further research:

1. Replication of this study for upper level African American administrators should be useful since these positions are important in relation to mobility of presidents.

2. A study that compares the career paths between senior level administrators of HBCUs and TWIs should provide further insights into the process of administrative career mobility.

3. Further studies should be conducted to evaluate the factors that keep women administrators out of the pool of candidates for presidency or negatively impact their selection.

4. Research should compare African American presidents and presidents of other minority groups to evaluate the trends and patterns pertaining to upward mobility.

5. This study should be replicated with a larger sample of African American presidents of traditionally white universities by using a different methodology.

6. An in-depth study of upward career mobility of presidents of HBCUs should be conducted in the context of institutional characteristics. Among these characteristics are differences in origin, that is, whether the institution was founded by a black or a white organization, and differences in the organizational affiliations and thus the independence of members of the boards of trustees. According to Jerome Green, these differences have historically led to differences in administrative actions and strategies, and could influence advancement of candidates to the presidency (Jerome Green, email to the author, April 20, 2006).

7. Research should be continued using internal labor market theory in HBCUs for providing a better understanding of the careers for African Americans aspiring to hold administrative positions.

References

Adams, R. L. 2001. Thirty years of black "firsts" in higher education. *The Black Collegian Magazine, 31*(3), 88-91.

Adler, E. S., and R. Clark. 1999. *How it's done: An invitation to social research.* New York: Wadsworth Publishing.

African American presidents of white colleges and universities: They broke through one of the last taboos in higher education. 2000. *The Journal of Black Issues in Higher Education, 28,* 94-97.

Allen, W. R., and J. O. Jewel. 2002. A backward glance forward: Past, present, and future perspectives on historically black colleges and universities. *The Review of Higher Education, 25*(3), 241-261.

Altbach, P., K. Lomotey, and S. Kyle. 1999. Race in higher education. In P. G. Altbach, R. O. Berdahl, and P. J. Gumport, eds. *American higher education in the 21st century* (pp. 448-466). Baltimore and London: John Hopkins University Press.

Althauser, R. P. 1989. Internal labor markets. *Annual Review of Sociology, 15,* 143-161.

Althauser, R., and A. Kalleberg. 1981. Firms, occupations, and the structure of labor markets: A conceptual analysis. In I. Berg (Ed.), *Sociological perspectives on labor markets.* New York: Academic Press.

Amey, M. J., K. E. Van DerLinden, and D. F. Brown. 2002. Perspectives on community college leadership. *Community College Journal of Research and Practice, 26,* 573-589.

Babbie, E. 2001. *The practice of social research.* Belmont, CA: Wadsworth/Thompson Learning.

Barwick, J. T. 2002. Pathways to presidency: Same trail, new vistas. *Community College Journal, 73*(1), 6-11.

Basinger, J. 2002. Staying power. *Chronicle of Higher Education, 49*(3), 28-30.

Bennefield, R. M. 1999. Trench warriors: On the front lines. *Black Issues in Higher Education, 16*(13), 69-79.

Bennett, Jr., L., ed. 1991. The new wave of college presidents. *Ebony, 47*(1), 27.

Bennett, L. et al., eds. 2001. *Who's who among African Americans, 14th edition.* Belmont, CA:The Gale Group.

Berg, B. L. 2001. *Qualitative research methods for the social sciences.* Boston: Allyn and Bacon.

Bills, D. B. 1987. Costs, commitment and rewards: Factors influencing the design and implementation of internal labor markets. *Administrative Science Quarterly, 32,* 202-221.

Birnbaum, R. 1999. The dilemma of presidential leadership. In P. G. Altbach, R. O. Berdahl, and P. J. Gumport, eds., *American higher education in the twenty-first century* (pp. 323-334). Baltimore: John Hopkins University Press.

Black college presidents: Pioneering on the frontiers of education. 2001. *Ebony, 56*(11), 126.

References

Blake, J. H., and E. L. Moore. 1999. The color line: The enduring challenge in higher education. *Metropolitan Universities: An International Forum, 9*, 77-80.

Blount, J. M. 1998. *Destined to rule the schools: Women and the superintendency, 1873-1995*. Albany, NY: State University of New York Press.

Bok, D. 1998. *Higher learning*. Boston, MA: Harvard University Press.

Boyan, N. J. 1988. Describing and explaining administrator behavior. In N. J. Boyan, (Ed.), *Handbook of research on educational administration: A project of the American Educational Research Association*. New York: Longman.

Brown, W. 1997. Increasing power, not just numbers. *Black Issues in Higher Education, 14*, 92-93.

Brown, L., M. Martinez, and D. Daniel. 2002. Community college leadership preparations: Needs, perceptions, and recommendations. *Community College Review, 30*(1), 45.

Bouchard, Jr., T. J. 1976. Unobtrusive measures: An inventory of uses. *Sociological Methods and Research, 4*, 267-300.

Castenada, C., M. Guitierrez, and S. G. Katsinas. 2002. *Community College Journal of Research and Practice, 26*, 297-314.

Chamberlain, M., ed. 1988. *Women in academe: Progress and prospects*. New York: Russell Sage Foundation.

Cohen, M., and J. March. 1974. *Leadership and ambiguity*. New York: McGraw-Hill.

Coleman, J. E. 1998. *Barrier to career mobility/advancement by African American and Caucasian female administrators in Minnesota organizations: A perception or reality?* ERIC Document Reproduction Service, No. ED 423590. Retrieved September 15, 2003, from http://www.edrs.com/.

Corrigan, M. E., ed. 2002. *The American college president: 2002 edition*. Washington, DC: American Council on Education Center for Policy Analysis.

Cortada, R. L. 1996. The powers of the presidency. In R. Bowen and G. Muller, eds., *Achieving administrative diversity*. San Francisco: Jossey-Bass.

Cunningham, J. J. 1992. *Black administrators as managers in higher education*. ERIC Document Reproduction Service, No. ED 342307. Retrieved September 15, 2003, from http://www.edrs.com/

Department of Agriculture. 1980. *White House report: Initiatives on historically black colleges and universities*. ERIC Document Reproduction Service, No. ED 315604. Retrieved September 15, 2003, from http://www.edrs.com/

Dill, D. D. 1984. The nature of administrative behavior in higher education. *Education Administration Quarterly, 20*(3), 69-99.

Drucker, P. 1966. *The effective executive*. New York: Harper Collins.

Duderstadt, J. J. 2000a. *Fire, ready, aim! University decision making during an era of rapid change*. La Jolla, CA: The Glion Colloquium II.

———. 2000b. *A university for the 21st century*. Ann Arbor: The University of Michigan Press.

Dunlop, J. 1966. Job vacancy measures and economic analysis. In National Bureau of Economic Research (Ed.), *The measurement and interpretation of job vacancies*. New York: National Bureau of Economic Research.

Elam, J. C., ed. 1989. *Blacks in higher education: Overcoming the odds*. Lanham, MD: NAFEO.

Esquibel, A. 1997. *The career mobility of Chicano administrators in higher education*. Boulder, CO: The Western Interstate Commission for Higher Education.

Evangelauf, J. 1984. Presidents say they're spending more time away from campuses. *Chronicle of Higher Education, 15*, 1.

References

Evelyn, J. 1998a. Black presidents. *Community College Week, 10(6),* 6.
———. 1998b. Climbing to the top. *Black Issues in Higher Education, 15,* 34-35.
Fairweather, J. 1996. *Faculty work and public trust: Restoring the value of teaching and public service in American academic life.* Boston: Allyn and Bacon.
Fincher, C. 1997. *Presidential qualifications and institutional structure.* Athens, GA: The University of Georgia Institute of Higher Education.
Fisher, J. L. 1984. *Power of the presidency.* New York: Macmillan.
Fisher, J., and M. Tack. 1990. The effective college president. *Educational Record, 71* 1.
Frierson, C. 1993. *Perceptions of African American educators toward historically black colleges and universities.* ERIC Documentation Service, No. ED 375193. Retrieved September 15, 2003, from http://www.edrs.com/
Garibaldi, A., ed. 1984. Paradox and promise: Leadership and the neglected minorities. *New Directions for Community Colleges, 24*(2), 5-12.
Glaser, B. G. 1968. Moving between organizations. In B. G. Glaser, ed., *Organizational careers: A sourcebook for theory.* Chicago: Aldine Publishing.
Gleason, Jan. 2000. Duderstadt predicts big changes in digital age. *Emory Report, 52*(25).
Gray III., W. H. 1997. *The case for all-black colleges.* Washington, DC: Washington Post Book World Service/Washington Post Writers Group.
Green, M. F., ed. 1988. *Leaders for a new era: Strategies for higher education.* New York: Macmillan.
———. 1988. *The American president: A contemporary profile.* ERIC Document Reproduction Services, No. ED 311747. Retrieved September 15, 2003, from http://www.edrs.com/
Green, M. F., assisted by M. Ross and E. Holmstrom. 1988 *The American college president: A contemporary profile.* Washington, DC: American Council on Education.
Griffiths, D. E. 1988. Administrative theory. In N. J. Boyan (Ed.), *Handbook on research on educational administration* (pp. 27-52). New York: Longman.
Gupton, S., and R. M. Del Rosario. 1997, March. *An analysis of federal initiatives to support women's upward mobility in educational administration.* Paper presented at the annual meeting of the American Educational Research Association, Chicago.
Hahn, R. 1995, September/October. Getting serious about presidential leadership. *Change,* 13-19.
Hall, D. T. 1976. *Careers in organizations.* Pacific Palisades, CA: Goodyear.
Harvey, W. B., ed. 1999. *Grassroots and glass ceilings: African American administrators in predominantly white colleges and universities.* New York: State University of New York Press.
Hawkins, D. B. 1995, January. AAUP report finds HBCU role essential to higher education: Fallout from Fordice at the heart of Study. *Black Issues in Higher Education.*
Heiman, G. W. 2000. *Basic statistics for the behavioral sciences* (3rd ed.). Boston: Houghton Mifflin.
Henderson, A. N., and J. M. York, eds. 2002. *Who's who among African Americans, 15th edition.* Belmont, CA: The Gale Group.
Henderson, J. L. 2001. HBCUs will still have a role to play in the 21st century. *Black Issues in Higher Education, 17*(25), 48.
The historically black colleges and universities: A future in the balance. 1995. *Academe, 81*(1), 49-58.
Hoffman, C. M., T. D. Snyder, and B. Sonnenberg. 1996. *Historically black colleges and universities, 1976-94.* Washington, DC: National Center for Education Statistics, U.S. Government Printing Office.

References

Institutions designated as Historically Black Colleges and Universities. 2000, March 6. Historically Black Colleges and Universities List. Retrieved September 19, 2002, from http://www.ed.gov/offices/OPE/HEP/idues/hbculist.html

Jones, L., ed. 2001. *Retaining African Americans in higher education.* Stylus.

Jones, S. 1995. The glass ceiling and African-American administrators in higher Education. *Dissertation Abstracts International, 56,* 08A.

Jusman, A. 1999. Issues facing higher education in the 21st century. In P. G. Altbach, R. O. Berdahl, and P. J. Gumport, eds., *American higher education in the 21st century* (pp. 109-148). Baltimore: The Johns Hopkins University Press.

Kauffman, J. F. 1980. *At the pleasure of the board: The service of the college and university president.* Washington, DC: American Council on Education.

Kelly, E. 2002. The changing of the guard. *Community College Week, 14,* 6-9.

Kerr, C., and M. L. Gade. 1986. *The many lives of academic presidents: Time, place, and character.* Washington, DC: Association of Governing Boards of Universities and Colleges.

King, S., and J. R. Chepyator. 1996. Factors affecting the enrollment and persistence of African-American doctoral students. *Physical Education, 53*(4), 170.

Kit, L. 2000. Diversity increases among presidents. *Chronicle of Higher Education, 47*(3).

Lamb, Y. R. 1989. Lighting the way for youth. *Black Enterprise, 19,* 205-207.

Lewin, R., and B. Regine, eds. 2001. Paradoxical leadership. In R. Lewin and B. Regine, eds., *Weaving complexity and business* (pp. 263-280). New York: Texere LLC.

Lindsey, B. 1994. African American women and Brown: A lingering twilight or emerging dawn? *Journal of Negro Education, 63*(3), 430-442. [Special issue, *Brown v. Board of Education* at 40: A commemorative issue dedicated to the late Thurgood Marshall.]

Lockett, G. C. 1994, March. *Empowerment in HBCUs and PBCUs: Developing microcosms of the beloved community through the re-definition of social institutions and the learning and application of values.* Paper presented at the Annual Conference of the National Association for Equal Opportunity in Higher Education, Washington, DC.

Lomotey, K. 1997. *Sailing against the wind: African Americans and women in U. S. education.* Albany, NY: State University of New York Press.

Lopez, Jr., B. 1996. Factors affecting the career mobility of upper-level Hispanic school administrators. *Equity and Excellence in Education, 29(3).*

McDade, Sharon A. 1988, June 1. Higher education leadership: Enhancing skills through professional development programs. *Ashe-Eric Higher Education Reports.*

McLure, G. T., A. M. S. Rao, and W. Lester. 1999. *Comparing student perceptions of general education and personal growth outcomes at HBCU and non-HBCU institutions.* ERIC Document Reproduction Service. Retrieved September 15, 2003, from http://www.edrs.com/

Mason, J. C. 1993. Women at work: Knocking on the glass ceiling. *Management Review, 5.*

Miklos, E. 1988. Administrator selection, career patterns, succession, and socialization. In N. J. Boyan, ed., *Handbook of research on educational administration.* New York: Longman.

Moore, K. M. 1984. Careers in college and university administration: How are women affected? In A. Tinsley, C. Secor, and S. Kaplan, eds., *Women in higher education administration,* New Direction for Higher Education Series No. 45. San Francisco: Jossey-Bass.

References

———. 1993a. *Leaders in transition: A national study of higher education administrators.* University Park: Center for the Study of Higher Education, Pennsylvania State University.

———. 1993b. The top-line: A report on presidents', provosts', and deans' careers. *Leaders in transition.* University Park: Pennsylvania State University and the American Council on Education. ERIC Document Reproduction Service. Retrieved September 15, 2003, from http: //www.edrs.com/

Moore, K. M., S. V. Martorana, and S. Twombley. 1985. *Today's academic leaders: A national study of administrators in two-year colleges.* University Park: Center for the Study of Higher Education, Pennsylvania State University.

Moore, K. M., A. M. Salimbene, and S. M. Bragg. 1983. The structure of presidents' and deans' careers. *Journal of Higher Education, 54,* 500-515.

Moore, M. 2000. Cracking the concrete ceiling: An inquiry into the aspirations, values, motives, and actions of African American female 1980 cooperative extension administrators. *Dissertations Abstracts International, 61(08A),* 3028.

Mosley, M. H. 1980. Black women administrators in higher education: An endangered species. *Journal of Black Studies, 3,* 295-310.

Myers, S. L., and W. J. Roscoe. 1994. *A status report of the HBCUs and NAFEO's EOEIS.* Washington, DC: NAFEO Research Institute.

NAFEO profile. 2002. Twenty-seventh National Conference on Blacks in Higher Education.

The National Advisory Committee on Black Higher Education and Black Colleges and Universities, 1. 1980. Washington, DC: U. S. Government Printing Office.

National Association for Equal Opportunity List of Member Institutions. 2002. Retrieved October 10, 2002, from http://www.nafeo.org/members.html

New York State Department of Education. 1997, June. *Preliminary report of the district superintendent's Committee on Women and Minority Administration.* New York: Author.

New Black College Presidents. 1999, Oct. *Ebony.* Retrieved November 8, 2002, from http://findarticles.com/cf_dls/m1077/12_54/55982847/print.jhtml

Nicholson, N., and M. A. West. 1988. *Managerial job change: Men and women in transition.* New York: Cambridge University Press.

Ortiz, F. I., and C. Marshall. 1988. Women in educational administration. In N. J. Boyan, ed., *Handbook of research on educational administration,* pp. 123-142. New York: Longman Publisher.

Penney, S. H. 1996, Spring/Summer. Five challenges for academic leaders in the 21st century. *The Educational Record,* 123-142.

Phelps, D. G., L. Taber, and C. Smith. 1996. African American community college presidents. *Community College Review, 24,* 3-26.

Quick reference to African American college and university presidents. 1998. *Black Issues in Higher Education, 15*(6), 18-19.

Ramey, F. H. 1995. Obstacles faced by African-American women administrators in higher education: How they cope. *The Western Journal of Black Studies, 19*(2), 113-119.

Rehfuss, J. 1984, June 27. What goes wrong (and sometimes right) with presidential searches. *Chronicle of Higher Education.*

Rhodes, F. 1998, Spring. The art of presidency. *The Presidency, 1,* 12-18.

Richards, C. 1988. The search for equity in educational administration: A commentary. In N. J. Boyan, ed., *Handbook of research on educational administration* (pp. 159-169). New York: Longman Publisher.

References

Richmond, P. A., and S. Maramark. 1996. *On the road to economic development: A guide for continuing education programs at HBCUs*. Washington, DC: Office of Educational Research and Improvement.

Ritchey, F. J. 2000. *The statistical imagination*. New York: McGraw-Hill.

Roach, R. 2000, May. Decisions of the head and heart. *Black Issues in Higher Education, 17*, 22-25.

Roebuck, J. B., and K. S. Murty. 1993. *Historically black colleges and universities: Their place in American higher education*. Westport, CT: Praeger.

Rolle, K. A., T. G. Davies, and J. H. Banning. 2000. African American administrators' experiences in predominantly white colleges and universities. *Community College Journal of Research and Practice, 24*(2), 79.

Rosenblatt, R. A. 1995, March 16. 'Glass ceiling' still too hard to crack, U. S. panel finds. *Los Angeles Times*.

Ross, M., and M. F. Green. 1990. The rules of the game: The unwritten code of career mobility. In K. M. Moore and S. B. Twombly, eds., *New directions for higher education,* pp. 67-77. San Francisco: Jossey-Bass.

Ross, M., and M. F. Green. 1993. *The American college president*. Washington, DC: American Council on Education.

———. 1998. *The American college president*. Washington, DC: American Council on Education.

Rudolph, R. 1990. *The American college and university: A history*. Athens, GA: The University of Georgia Press.

Sandler, B. R. 1979. You've come a long way maybe— or why it still hurts to be a woman in labor. In American Association for Higher Education (Ed.), Employment practices in academe. *Current Issues in Higher Education Monograph, 4*.

Santiago, I. S. 1996. Increasing the Latino leadership pipeline: Institutional and organizational strategies. In R. C. Bowen and G. H. Muller, eds., *New Directions for Community Colleges, 24*(99).

Scott, M. 2002, September 2. Black colleges losing presidents. *The Salt Lake Tribune*. Retrieved January 18, 2003, from www.sltrib.com/2002/sep/09212002/ nation_w/ 183502.htm

Sechrest, L. 1980. *Unobtrusive measurement today*. San Francisco: Jossey-Bass.

Shapesaft, C. 1999 The struggle to create a more gender-inclusive profession. In J. Murphy and K. S. Louis, eds., *Handbook of research on educational administration*. San Francisco: Jossey-Bass.

Shea, R. H. 2003, September 1. How we got here. *U. S. News and World Report, 135*.

Sims, S. 1994. *Diversifying historically black colleges and universities: A new higher education paradigm*. ERIC Document Reproduction Service, No. ED 375765. Retrieved September 15, 2003, from http://www.edrs.com/

Smith, C. H. 1981. *The predominantly black college: An exploration of its role and function*. ERIC Document Reproduction Service, No. ED 207409. Retrieved September 15, 2003, from http://www.edrs.com/

Smolansky, B. 1984. *Job transition behavior in the labor market for administrators in higher education*. Unpublished doctoral dissertation, The Pennsylvania State University, University Park.

Steward, D. W. 1984. *Secondary research: Information sources and methods*. Beverly Hills, CA:Sage.

Suggs, E. 1997. *HBCUs getting up to speed on the information highway*. ERIC Document Reproduction Service, No. ED 547669. Retrieved September 15, 2003, from http://www.edrs.com/

References

Sutton, W. W. 1994, August. *Remarks prepared for NAFEO Presidential Peer Seminar*, Hilton Head, SC.

Taliaferro, B. M., and A. L. Montoya. 1995. *Faculty and administrators of color in the Pennsylvania state system of higher education: A status report.* ERIC Document Reproduction Service, No. ED 381504. Retrieved September 15, 2003, from http://www.edrs.com/

Thomas, A. E., and R. L. Green. 1993, August. HBCUs: An irreplaceable national treasure.

Thompson, D. C. 1973. *Private black colleges at the crossroads.* West Port, CT: Greenwood Press.

Thompson, J. D., R. W. Avery, and R. O. Carlson. 1968. Occupations, personnel, and careers. *Education Administration Quarterly, 4*, 6-31.

Torregrosa, C. H. 2002. *Higher education directory.* Falls Church, VA: Higher Education Publications.

Townsend, B. K. 1996. The role of the professoriate in influencing the community college leadership. In J. C. Palmer and S. G. Katsinas, eds., *Graduate and continuing education for community college leaders: What it means today* (pp. 59-64). San Francisco: Jossey-Bass.

Turner, B. 2002. HBCUs: An educational system at the crossroads. *Black Issues in Higher Education, 19*(14), 50.

Twombly, S. B. 1986a. Boundaries of an administrative labor market. *Community College Review, 13*, 34-44.

———. 1986b. *Career lines of top-level two-year college administrators: Implications for leadership in a new era.* Paper presented at the annual meeting of the Association for the Study of Higher Education, San Antonio, TX. ERIC Document Reproduction Service, No. ED 268884. Retrieved September 15, 2003, from http://www.edrs.com/

———. 1988. Administrative labor market. *Journal of Higher Education, 59*(6), 668-689.

United Negro College Fund—Member Map. 2001. Retrieved February 2, 2003, from http://www.uncf.org/

U. S. Census Bureau. 2001. American fact-finder. Data File, U. S. Census Bureau. Retrieved September 15, 2003, from www.census.govq

Valverde, L. A., and F. Brown. 1988. Influences on leadership development among racial and ethnic minorities. In N. J. Boyan (Ed.), *Handbook of research on education administration* (pp. 143-158). New York: Longman.

Vander Woerdt, L. 1992. *Affirmative action in higher education.* New York: Garland.

Vardi, Y. 1980. Organizational career mobility: An integrative model. *Academy of Management Review, 5*, 341-355.

Vaughan, G. B. 1990. *Pathways to the presidency: Community college dean or instruction.* Washington, DC: The Community College Press.

———. 1996. Paradox and promise: Leadership and the neglected minorities. In R. Bowen and G. Muller,eds. San Francisco: Jossey-Bass.

Vaughan, G. B., and I. M. Weisman. 1998. *The community college presidency at the millennium.* ERIC Document Reproduction Service, No. ED 417789. Retrieved September 15, 2003, from http://www.edrs.com/

Warner, R. L., and L. B. Defleur. Career paths of women in higher education administration. In P. T. Mitchell, ed., *Cracking the glass wall: Women in higher education administration.* Washington, DC: The College and University Personnel Association.

Wessel, R. D., and M. Keim. 1994. Career patterns of private four-year college and university presidents in the United States. *Journal of Higher Education, 65*(2), 211-225.

White House Initiative on Historically Black Colleges and Universities. 1997. *Historically black colleges and universities for the 21st Century: Annual report of the President's Board of Advisors on Historically Black Colleges and Universities.* Washington, DC: Department of Education.

Whiting, A. N. 1991. *Guardians of the flame: Historically black colleges yesterday, today, and tomorrow.* Washington, DC: American Association of State Colleges and Universities.

Who will lead higher education's transformation? 1997, Fall. *Planning for Higher Education, 26,* 50-54.

Who's Who in America. 2002. Chicago: A. N. Marquis.

Wilensky, H. 1960. Orderly careers and social participation: The impact of work history on social integration in the middle mass. *American Sociological Review, 26,* 521-539.

Williams, D. 1988.*The closure crisis at Mississippi Valley State University: 1982-1986.* Unpublished Doctoral Dissertation, Southern Illinois University.

Wilson, G. 1997. Pathways to power: Racial differences in the determinants of job authority. *Social Problems, 44,* 38-54.

Wilson, R. 1990. Can black colleges solve problems of access for black students? *American Journal of Education, 98*(4), 443-457.

———. 1996, Summer. The unfinished agenda. *New Direction for Community Colleges,* 93-99.

Zusman, A. 1999. Issues facing higher education in the 21st century. In P. Altbach, R. Berdahl, and P. Gumport, eds., *American higher education in the twenty-first century* (pp. 323-334). Baltimore: Johns Hopkins University Press.

Index

academic discipline
   as independent variable, 5, 6, 37, 42
   relative to mobility, 43, 61, 63
   implications in career planning, 71
additional training
   as independent variable, 5
   relative to mobility, 44-45, 62
   resources for, as part of compensation package, 71
administrative experience. *See* experience, professional
African American college and university presidents, 8
   compared with white counterparts, 1, 5, 47
African American students, 4, 7, 8, 24-25
   enrollment at HBCUs, 25
African American women in higher education.
   as administrators, 19-20
   See also women in higher education
African Methodist Episcopal Church, 22
age, 15
   as independent variable, 5, 37, 45, 48, 64-65
   relative to mobility, 46, 48-49
American Association of University Presidents (AAUP), 25
American Council of Education (ACE), 15, 17, 20, 30, 31
analysis of data, 37-57

ancillary analysis, 56-57
ancillary findings, 70
Annual Report of the President's Board on Historically Black Colleges and Universities, 15
archival sources, 5, 9
assumptions, 7

biographical data, 5, 7, 37
Black Issues in Higher Education, 25
board of trustees, 7
Brown v. Board of Education of Topeka, Kansas (1954), 24

career
   definition of, 6
   profile of college and university presidents, 5, 37; 39-40, 60-62
career entry position. *See* entry position
career ladder, 2
career mobility
   definition of, 6
   and internal labor markets, 27-29, 68-70
career mobility model, 2
Carnegie Commission on Higher Education, 25
chi-square tests, 35, 37, 42, 43-47, 55, 57
civic organizations. *See* professional and civic organizations
Civil Rights era, 17, 61
Civil War, 23
Clinton, Bill, 4
Clinton Administration, 23

community college presidents, 15
community colleges, 15, 18
community organizations. *See* professional and civic organizations
conceptual/theoretical framework, 26-29
cross-tabulation analysis, 35, 37, 43, 44, 45, 46, 47, 55, 56, 60

data cleaning, 35
definitions, 6
degrees earned
　as educational variable, 37; 39; 52, 61
　institution awarding, 50-51
delimitation of the study, 7
demographic profile, 37-42, 60-62, 65-68
demographic variables, 4, 37
descriptive statistics, 35; 60
diversity, 3, 16
Dubois, W. E. B., 23
Duderstadt, James W., 12
Dunster, Henry, 11

educational discipline. *See* academic discipline
educational profile of African American college and university presidents, 39, 41
educational variables, 4, 37, 60-62, 66
entry position
　as independent variable, 6, 15, 27, 46, 53, 54, 62, 65
　relative to mobility, 47
European and Asian presidents, 12
European model of presidency, 1
experience, professional
　administrative, 54, 71
　at HBCUs, 52, 62, 66
　at non-HBCUs, 53
　faculty, 62, 65

faculty experience. *See under* experience, professional
fields of study. *See* academic discipline
findings associated with career mobility/labor market components, 68
first administrative position. *See* entry position

gender
　as independent variable, 5, 15, 37, 48, 57, 63-64
　relative to academic discipline, 43-44, 63
　relative to marital status, 57
　relative to mobility, 43, 44, 56, 63
gender gap, 5, 61, 63-64, 70
　See also glass ceiling
glass ceiling, 21, 63, 71
"Good Old Boy" network, 21
Gray, William, III, 22, 24

HBCUs. *See* Historically Black Colleges and Universities (HBCUs)
Higher Education Act of 1965, 22
Higher Education Directory, 35
Hispanic population, 1
Hispanic-serving institutions, (HSIs), 17
Hispanic students, 18
Hispanics in higher education, 18-19,
historical overview, 22-24
Historically Black Colleges and Universities (HBCUs),
　definition of, 6
　importance of, 2
　history of, 22-24
holistic disciplines, 71
"human capital," 69
hypotheses, 5

implications for policy and practice, 71
institutional type

as independent variable, 39, 41, 50-51
relative to mobility, 56
internal labor market theory, 3, 29-30, 72
see also career mobility
implications for policy and practice, 71
institutional culture, 28-29, 62
inter-institutional mobility, 29
institutional traditions. See institutional culture
institutions, type of, 66
introduction, 1-9

leadership effectiveness, 1
limitation of the study, 7
Lincoln University, 22
Lindsey, Beverly, 24
longevity issues, 2, 15
management related training, see training beyond terminal degree
marital status
as independent variable, 5, 16, 45, 61, 64-65, 70
relative to mobility rates, 46, 57
Massey, Walter, 4
materials, 33-34
mentoring, 62
methodology, 31-35; 60
minorities in higher education, 1
minority presidents in higher education, 16
mobility
definition of, 6
patterns of, 2, 28
mobility rate
as dependent variable, 2
definition of, 32
Morril Acts, 23

NAFEO
See National Association for Equal Opportunity (NAFEO)

National Association for Equal Opportunity (NAFEO)
definition, 6
National Association for Equal Opportunity (NAFEO) Research Institute, 22, 26, 34-35
National Center for Education Statistics, 22, 24
Nelson, Dr. Ivory, 17
networking, 62, 63
normative career ladder. See career ladder

organizational/structural level of analysis, 3

Paradoxical Leadership model, 14
participants, 32-33
patterns of mobility. See under mobility
Pearson chi square test. See chi square test
Penny, Sherry, 13
post-doctoral training. See training beyond terminal degree
Presidency, The , 15
presidents in higher education, 1, 11-12; 26
procedures, 34-35
professional and civic organizations
leadership positions in, 55
membership in, 42, 53; 62, 67
professional development, 71
See also additional training
professional experience. See experience, professional
professional mobility
definition of, 6
See also mobility
psychological and social concepts, 28
public archival sources, 37
purpose of the study, 4

qualitative aspects of the study, 31, 35

race and gender issues in higher education, 16-22, 71-72
  See also minorities in higher education, women in higher education, minority presidents in higher education
recommendations for future research, 71-72
region of origin
  as independent variable 5, 38-39, 45, 49, 61, 64,
  relative to mobility rate, 47
review of literature, 11-30
research design, 31-32
research findings, 60-68
research questions, 5, 37
research question 1, 37, 60
research question 2, 42, 43, 63
research question 3, 43, 63-64
research question 4, 44-45, 64
research question 5, 45-46, 63-64
research question 6, 46-47, 65
research question 7, 47-56, 65-68
review of literature, 11-30; 60
Richards, Craig, 21
role of HBCUs, 24-25
role of presidency, 1

Search for Equity in Educational Administration, 21
selection process, 71
Shea, Rachel Hartigan, 12
significance of the study, 7-9
societal changes, 1
summary, 59-61
support systems, 4
statement of the problem, 3-4
Statistical Packages for the Social Sciences (SPSS), 35
students: attitude study, 25
success criteria, 1, 2, 4
summary 59-60
summary, conclusions, implications, and recommendations, 59-72

support system, 2
theoretical framework, 2-3
traditionally white institutions (TWIs)
  presidents of, 1, 6, 35, 48-57
turnover rates. See longevity
TWIs. See traditionally white institutions

"Unforgettable Presidential Moments," 17
United Negro College Fund (UNCF), 23, 33
University Faculty Voice, The, 33
unobtrusive methods
  definition of, 6
  use in the study, 33
upward professional mobility
  definition of, 6, 26
  comparison between presidents of HBCUs and TWIs, 47-56
  dearth of literature in field of higher education, 11
  minority populations and, 11
  relative to additional training beyond terminal degree, 44-45, 64
  relative to academic disciplines, 43-44
  relative to entry position, 46-47, 65
  relative to gender, 43-44, 63-64
  relative to marital status, age, and state of origin, 45-46, 64-65

validity of the source material, 33-34

Washington, Booker T., 23
White House Initiative on HBCUs, 23
Wilberforce University, 22
Who's Who among African Americans, 6, 34
women and minority presidents in community colleges, 18
women in higher education, 16-22